TEEN SEX

Other books in the At Issue series:

TEEN SEX

Tamara L. Roleff, *Book Editor*

Daniel Leone, *President*
Bonnie Szumski, *Publisher*
Scott Barbour, *Managing Editor*

An Opposing Viewpoints® Series

Greenhaven Press, Inc.
San Diego, California

Library of Congress Cataloging-in-Publication Data

Teen sex / Tamara L. Roleff, book editor.
    p. cm. — (At issue)
  Includes bibliographical references and index.
  ISBN 0-7377-0808-5 (pbk. : alk. paper) —
ISBN 0-7377-0809-3 (lib. : alk. paper)
    1. Teenagers—United States—Sexual behavior. 2. Sex instruction for teenagers—United States. 3. Hygiene, Sexual—United States. 4. Sexual ethics for teenagers—United States.
I. Roleff, Tamara L., 1959– II. At issue (San Diego, Calif.)

HQ27 .T394   2002
306.7'0835—dc21   2001040357
                                                              CIP

© 2002 by Greenhaven Press, Inc.
10911 Technology Place, San Diego, CA 92127

Printed in the U.S.A.

Table of Contents

Introduction

The teen birthrate declined steadily throughout much of the 1990s. In 1999, the last year for which records are available, the birthrate among teens aged fifteen to nineteen dropped to a record low of 49.6 births per 1,000. The 1999 teen birthrate is the lowest it has been since the National Center for Health Statistics began keeping records in 1940. The rate, which declined every year during the 1990s, fell 3 percent in 1999 and has fallen 20 percent since 1991. The 20-percent decrease has effectively erased the 24-percent increase in teen births from 1986 (50.2 per 1,000) to 1991, when teen births were 62.1 per 1,000.

Many sex researchers and commentators hail the declining teen birthrate as an indication of teens' changing values and beliefs about premarital sex. They believe "abstinence-only" sex education programs—classes in which students are taught only about the benefits of abstinence with no mention of birth control or "safe sex"—are having an effect on teen sexual behaviors. "More teens are choosing abstinence," contends Janet Parshall of the Family Research Council, an organization that promotes the traditional family. She asserts that tens of thousands of teens have pledged to remain virgins until marriage in abstinence programs such as True Love Waits. A survey conducted for the National Campaign to Prevent Teen Pregnancy (NCPTP) seems to support her contention that more teens are deciding to remain abstinent. According to the 2000 survey, 58 percent of teenagers believe high-school teens should not engage in sexual activity, even if precautions are taken against pregnancy or sexually transmitted diseases (STDs). An overwhelming majority—93 percent—said they believe society should tell teens to remain abstinent at least until they graduate from high school. The survey also found that half of the teens said that fear of pregnancy or STDs is the main reason they are abstinent. In addition, the vast majority of teens—87 percent—do not think it is embarrassing to admit that they are virgins.

Perhaps due in part to the message emphasizing abstinence, fewer teens are having sex. According to the NCPTP, the number of male teens who have had sex declined from 61 percent in 1990 to 49 percent in 1997. The number of teen girls who have had sex has fluctuated: 48 percent in 1990, up to 52 percent in 1995, and back down again to 48 percent in 1997.

Abstinence-only programs frequently stress the consequences of premarital sex: pregnancy and STDs, including HIV/AIDS. Donna E. Shalala, secretary of Health and Human Services under President Bill Clinton, believes that a fear of contracting AIDS has persuaded many teens to postpone sexual activity. "We all believe AIDS has scared teenagers," she says. Teens have a right to be scared: They have the fastest-increasing rate of HIV infection in the United States. Approximately 25 percent of the 40,000 new HIV infections reported annually occur among youth aged thirteen to twenty-one. Another 3 million teens aged thirteen to nineteen contract new STD infections each year.

Others contend that the falling birthrate is due to increased use of birth control by teens. They assert that partial credit for the increase in contraceptive use among teens can be given to school programs that distribute free condoms to students who request them. Studies comparing sexually active students in schools that provide condoms with schools that do not found that students were significantly more likely to use condoms during intercourse if they could get them at school.

A few studies and anecdotal evidence suggest to sex researchers that another reason the birthrate among teens is dropping is the increasing prevalence of oral sex as a substitute for intercourse. A 1999 survey by Planned Parenthood reported that 10 percent of teens who described themselves as virgins had had oral sex, some in their early teens. Other researchers contend that as many as one-third of middle-school girls are performing oral sex on boys. (Most experts agree that oral sex is not reciprocal—it is almost always boys who are the recipients.) However, researchers find it difficult to accurately determine whether the prevalence of oral sex is indeed increasing as many surveys about teen sexual behavior—past and present—concentrate solely on vaginal intercourse.

Some experts theorize that the increase in oral sex—if, indeed, there is one—is because many teens do not consider oral sex to be "sex." According to Peter Sheras, professor of adolescent development at the University of Virginia, oral sex "might mean what a French kiss meant to us when we were kids." Some teens even believe they are practicing abstinence if they engage in oral sex instead of sexual intercourse. Many adults are also not clear on whether oral sex is a form of abstinence. A 1999 survey even found that one-third of health educators believed that oral sex was abstinent behavior. President Bill Clinton, when answering questions regarding his affair with White House intern Monica Lewinsky, conveyed a similar attitude when he stated that they had not had "sexual relations" since they had engaged in oral sex.

Many parents and sex educators omit discussions about oral sex when telling teens about sex, and at least some experts believe this is a mistake. Linda Alexander, president of the American Social Health Association, believes that society has "drilled the kids on the dangers of pregnancy" but has not "talked as much about activities that don't result in pregnancy," such as oral sex. Many teens, especially younger teens who are not as well informed, believe—incorrectly—that they cannot contract STDs via oral sex. "What concerns me," Alexander continues, "is what kids don't know. They're not protecting themselves; they don't understand the risks of transmitting infection between the genital and oral areas."

It also appears that a larger number of teens than before are engaging in forms of sexual activity other than vaginal intercourse. Gary J. Gates and Freya L. Sonenstein reported in the November/December 2000 *Family Planning Perspectives* that although 55 percent of teen boys aged fifteen to nineteen reported that they had engaged in sexual intercourse in 1995, "two-thirds have had experience with noncoital behaviors like oral sex, anal intercourse, or masturbation by a female." In contrast, in 1988 less than half—40 percent—reported having ever been masturbated by a female. "These behaviors put kids at risk of getting sexually transmitted diseases," she notes. Gates and Sonenstein urge that teens be taught the risks of sexual activities other than intercourse and that researchers continue to monitor all forms of teens' sexual behavior.

Other experts on sexual behavior are also concerned about the high number of teens who believe themselves to be abstinent while engaging in oral and anal sex. These authorities believe that more attention needs to be paid to such behaviors. Ward Cates, president of the Family Health Institute and past director of the Division of Sexually Transmitted Diseases at the Centers for Disease Control and Prevention, asserts that parents and sex educators must get away from "the view that sex is vaginal intercourse and abstinence is nothing beyond holding hands."

Teens and adults agree that communication about values and sexual behavior—what is abstinence and what is sex and how to enjoy it safely— is necessary to promote teen abstinence. Studies have found that parental views on premarital sex are the most important influence on a teen's decision to remain abstinent. *Teen Sex: At Issue* examines the issue and extent of teen sexuality and explores various influences on a teen's decision to remain abstinent or become sexually active.

1

Premarital Teen
Sex Is Normal

Eric Zorn

Eric Zorn is a columnist for the Chicago Tribune.

A survey by a bridal magazine found that most men and women
were not virgins when they married. Abstinence-only sex education
programs maintain that premarital sex is immoral and unhealthy,
but in reality, most married couples have engaged in premarital sex
and do not regret it. Although trying to persuade teens to wait until marriage before they have sex, or at least delay it until they are
older, is a worthy goal, premarital sex is standard, normal behavior.

Readers of *Bride's* may be an unusually randy bunch, so we must use
some caution in approaching the results of the magazine's wedding-
night survey published in its August/September 1998 issue.

Out of 3,000 engaged couples who responded, just 4 percent of the
women and 1 percent of the men reported that they will be virgins when
they exchange vows. For women, the figure was down from 14 percent in
a similar *Bride's* survey in 1988, and on average, the women in 1998 reported having had six other sex partners aside from their husbands-to-be.

More scientific surveys have put the wedding-virginity rate at 7 to 16
percent for men and 20 to 30 percent for women, but either way the
numbers suggest two things:

1. The federal guidelines for abstinence-only education—a fad
pushed by social and religious conservatives and funded generously by
taxpayers—are based on wishful thinking.

2. The "But what did you do, mom and dad?" question about sex is
going to be even more awkward for today's parents than the same question has been about illegal-drug usage.

The guidelines for state programs taking advantage of the $50 million
Congress now allocates annually for no-sex education say teachers must
tell students that "abstinence from sexual activity outside marriage (is)

the expected standard . . . (and) that a mutually faithful monogamous relationship in the context of marriage is the expected standard of human sexual activity."

A standard practice

In reality, however, pre-marital and non-marital sex are standard practice in this country. An expectation that the man and woman you see standing at an altar or in front of a justice of the peace have never had sex is likely to be crushed by the truth.

Abstinence-only backers respond that "standard" here refers to a moral requirement, not a mathematical result or popularity poll. Premarital sex is bad, they say. Or, in the language of the federal guidelines: "Sexual activity outside the context of marriage is likely to have harmful psychological and physical effects."

But what did you do, mom and dad? Survey says . . . you probably indulged in the deed without the benefit of clergy at least a time or two. And it's my guess you weren't just "experimenting," the No. 1 old drug-use dodge, and you'd be less than candid if you said that you consider it all "a mistake," the No. 2 dodge.

Sometimes it was a mistake, of course. Sexuality is a complicated thing—dynamite in all metaphorical senses. When it explodes in your face, it's often because you misunderstood it, yourself or someone else.

When it doesn't explode, it can take you to new levels of intimacy where you learn valuable lessons about yourself and gain some of the perspective necessary for wisdom. This comes in handy later when you're pondering lifelong commitments.

Through such relationships you can learn what sex is and what it isn't; who you are and who you are not. Speaking for myself—one who belongs in the mainstream of *Bride's* readership, so to speak—I have regrets about certain indiscretions and related pain both received and inflicted. But overall I consider it to have been a real plus that I did not enter my now 13-year "faithful monogamous relationship in the context of marriage" as a virgin.

What to tell the kids?

What to tell the kids? They can smell hypocrisy at 100 yards, and "just say no" coming from an experienced generation that just said "oh, yes" is not likely to be persuasive, even in an age when sexually transmitted diseases pose a greater threat than in the past.

Yet that very experience also tells what we can say without reservation: Delay, restraint, moderation, contraception, love and respect are key elements of sexual responsibility. Holding off until at least the late teen years is by far the wisest choice.

Abstinence is a fine idea. It was never presented as an option to students in my schools in the 1970s, and it should have been.

But "abstinence-only" is an opinion. And, as today's brides and grooms tell us, a minority opinion at that.

2

Teen Sex Is Not Acceptable

Nancy Jergins

Nancy Jergins is the director of communications for Family First, an organization dedicated to raising awareness about the importance of families in society.

Premarital teen sex was once the exception, not the rule, in American society. Today, however, magazines, television, and movies feature and glamorize teen promiscuity. Teens are frequently emotionally unready for the responsibilities and risks inherent in sex. Unless parents begin to take charge and teach teens that premarital sex is unacceptable behavior, society will have to deal with the misery of brokenhearted and ailing children.

You may find this hard to believe, but there was a time when teenage sex was the exception, not the rule.

Sex sells

Of course, today, teen sex proudly stands fists on hips, smack in the middle of the public consciousness. In soap operas, it's a plot line. On MTV it's a *Real World,* real life, bisexual story line. And in magazines it's a talking point and a selling point.

The August [1993] cover of *YM* teases, "Passion Pointers from Crazy-in-Love Couples." For a seamless segue from prom to promiscuity, there's *CosmoGIRL!*—a new magazine for those too young for the worldly ways of *Cosmopolitan.* And *Jane* magazine's latest is the "Sex-Obsessed" issue.

On the more masculine side, there's *RAW,* a magazine about professional wrestling that hypes sex stereotypes and simulated sex acts glorified in the ring.

Just about every form of printed and spoken word, it seems, is pushing the "sex sells" envelope at the expense of our young people.

Reprinted from "Plain Talk: Teen Sex Is Not OK," by Nancy Jergins, *Christian Science Monitor,* August 6, 1999. Copyright © 1999 by Family First. Used with permission.

That's bad enough; what's worse is the way parents, who are supposed to look out for the best interest of their children, are instead giving in to the trend by allowing kids to go along with it.

When a sexually vulgar teen movie like *American Pie* causes stampedes at the box office, you have to wonder, "Maybe this is what the public wants."

Well, it may be what the public wants—but is it what the public needs?

It's time for parents to face and assess the impact of this sexually charged cultural environment, by asking themselves if anything good has come out of it.

If statistics don't lie, the answer would have to be, "no."

Every year in the United States, 3 million teenagers get a sexually transmitted disease. Even with easy access to birth control, 1 million teenage girls became pregnant last year.

Parents must tell teenagers that sex is rarely as glamorous and fallout-free as the sexual encounters shown on TV or in movies.

Even if contraception was 100 percent effective and teens used it 100 percent of the time, and even if you could take away the obvious physical consequences of sex, as the old song goes, "How can you mend a broken heart?"

A 14-year-old girl in the August 1999 issue of *Jump* magazine reflects on her decision to have sex. "I got very depressed. I was not ready on any level and got caught up in keeping my boyfriend happy."

She then asks other teenage girls, "How are you going to feel after the breakup (which will happen)? How many more guys will you give your body to? Those guys are gone from your life . . . but you will always be with your body, your mind, and your heart."

Boys can also suffer long-term emotional consequences from sex. A grown man who chose to abort his child before he was married still carries the scars.

"The regret, frustration, anger and loss are intense," he told a reporter recently. "As you progress through life . . . the loss of the child . . . does not go away."

Parents must speak out

Realizations like those are why parents must tell teenagers that sex is rarely as glamorous and fallout-free as the sexual encounters shown on TV or in movies, and it's not a shortcut to intimacy or being loved.

We need to teach teens about all of the risks associated with sex.

When it comes to sex, teenagers have the idealism of youth, as should be expected. So it's up to responsible adults to educate and protect them from the culture's dangerous, flippant take on adolescent sex.

Let's put aside personal crusades, political agendas, and the possibility of fast money, and truly look out for the best interest of our children.

The Spanish philosopher Jose Ortega y Gasset said, "Order is not a pressure which is imposed on society from without, but an equilibrium which is set up from within."

We must regain order within the sexual realm.

If we don't, then aside from the misery measured in statistics, we'll have to deal with the adolescent casualties of broken hearts, broken spirits, and yes, broken bodies.

We'll also have to be prepared to hear more world-weary 14-year-olds say of their first sexual encounter, "It was the saddest moment of my life."

3

The Rate of Teen Sex Is Declining

Richard T. Cooper

Richard T. Cooper is a staff reporter for the Los Angeles Times.

A government study found that for the first time since data has been collected, the percentage of teens who have had intercourse has declined. In 1970, the first year teen sex was surveyed, only 29 percent of teen girls aged fifteen to nineteen acknowledged having had sex. That figure increased to 55 percent in 1990, and dropped to 50 percent in 1997. The decline is similar for teen boys: 55 percent have had intercourse at least once in 1997, down from 60 percent in 1990. The survey also indicated more teens are using contraception. Some researchers attribute the changes to widespread sex education programs and more conservative attitudes among teens toward premarital sex.

For the first time in more than 20 years, there is evidence that the rising wave of premarital sexual intercourse among America's teenagers finally may have crested and begun to subside.

The first decline

New survey data released by the government show a decline in the percentage of unmarried teenagers of both sexes who acknowledged having had intercourse at some point between the ages of 15 and 19. These were the first declines ever recorded since the collection of such data began in the 1970s.

A large-scale study conducted in 1995 by the National Center for Health Statistics found that 50% of females 15 to 19 years old—married and unmarried—reported having had intercourse at least once, down from 55% in 1990. Fewer than 10% of those surveyed had been married. A parallel survey conducted for the government by the Urban Institute in 1995 showed a similar change among never-married male teenagers: 55% of males between 15 and 19 years of age said that they had had intercourse at some point, down from 60% in 1988.

"We welcome the news that the long-term increase in teenage sexual activity may finally have stopped," Health and Human Services Secretary Donna Shalala said in announcing the new data during a speech in Los Angeles on Thursday. "Continual increases in teen sexual activity are not inevitable."

Shalala and others called for a redoubling of efforts to reduce teen sexual activity, including a stronger message from adult society that teen sex is not acceptable. "We need to change the cultural messages that have been accepted too long," Shalala said.

New survey data . . . show a decline in the percentage of unmarried teenagers of both sexes who acknowledged having had intercourse.

The magnitude of the rise in teen sexual activity is reflected in the fact that in 1970, the year the health statistics center began its periodic surveys, only 29% of all females 15 to 19 reported having ever had sex.

"It was going up, and it didn't just plateau, it dropped. And that's good," said Kristin Moore, executive director of Child Trends Inc., a Washington-based research organization. "It changes the number of adolescents at risk by hundreds of thousands" for sexually transmitted diseases and for teen pregnancy.

"The longer kids delay, the better," she said.

Contraceptive use

The survey also showed a steep increase in the use of contraceptive devices—particularly condoms—by teenage girls during first-time intercourse. Fifteen years ago, the survey found, half of all female teenagers used some form of contraception the first time they had sex. In the 1990s, fully three-quarters reported doing so.

The number of female teenagers reporting that they had received formal training in using birth control, avoiding HIV and other sexually transmitted diseases and resisting pressure to have sex rose sharply as well.

Specialists attributed the decline in teen sex to a variety of factors, including fear of AIDS, more widespread sex education and changes in society's moral values.

A link with moral standards

One of those who linked changes in teen sexual activity to more emphatic moral standards in U.S. society was William Galston, a professor of public policy at the University of Maryland and board member of the National Campaign Against Teen Pregnancy. "There has been an important cultural shift in the last 10 years, relegitimizing the possibility of some moral judgments," he said.

The National Campaign to Prevent Teen Pregnancy seeks to cut teen pregnancy rates by one-third by 2005 by supporting stronger messages on values and a broad array of community-based anti-pregnancy programs.

Gracie Hsu, a health policy analyst at the Family Research Center, attributed the changes primarily to what she said are more conservative values among today's teenagers, who have seen the consequences—from heartache to sexually transmitted diseases—of early sex.

"It's important to recognize that this isn't happening in a vacuum," she said. "It isn't happening just because of sex education."

The role of sex education

But sex education has played a significant role. In 1995, more than 95% of 18- and 19-year-old females said that they had received formal instruction in practicing safe sex, avoiding HIV infection and other aspects of sexual behavior. Fewer than two-thirds of females who went through school only a few years earlier had received such training.

"The likely response to those kinds of education would be to postpone sex and use condoms, and that's exactly what we found," health statistics center statistician William Mosher said. "Obviously there were a lot of other things going on in the society, but this is one we can measure."

In a related development, the Alan Guttmacher Institute released new data showing that California led all states in teenage pregnancy, with 159 per 1,000 females ages 15 to 19. North Dakota was lowest with 59 per 1,000. Almost 8 of 10 teen pregnancies now occur outside marriage, the institute said.

The Guttmacher Institute, a private research organization, said that nationwide there are 112 pregnancies per 1,000 teenagers each year. Of these, 61 end in births, 36 in abortions and 15 in miscarriages.

4

Teens Are in the Midst of an STD Epidemic

Robyn Davis

Robyn Davis is the director of the Community Outreach and Education Division of the Los Angeles County Sexually Transmitted Disease Program.

Teens have the highest rate of sexually transmitted diseases of any age group. One reason teens are particularly susceptible to STDs is that many do not use a condom during sex. Teens are also frequently ignorant of the facts about sexually transmitted diseases and do not know how to prevent infection or where to go for treatment if they become infected.

Teens are deluged with images about sex. On TV alone, it is estimated that the average teen sees 14,000 sexual messages each year, less than 1% of which deal with sexual responsibility or consequences, according to a definitive study by Planned Parenthood. Unfortunately, thousands of teens face the very real consequences of sexually transmitted diseases (STDs) every day.

By the 12th grade, nearly two-thirds of U.S. high school students have had sexual intercourse, and approximately one-quarter have had four or more sex partners, according to a report done in recent years by the federal Centers for Disease Control and Prevention. Yet almost half of sexually active teens did not use a condom the last time they had sex, the report said.

An STD epidemic

The math is elementary: Sex minus condoms equals today's teen STD epidemic. Teens 15 to 19 have the highest rates of gonorrhea and chlamydia of any age group in Los Angeles County, and account for nearly one-third of all reported STD cases. Recent studies have found that nearly 10% of girls in some L.A. County high schools are infected with chlamydia. Other studies have found similar rates of human papillomavirus (HPV), the virus that causes genital warts, in teen girls.

Teens are particularly susceptible to STDs for several reasons. Many know little about the STDs that most commonly affect them. Instead, misconceptions abound, such as: "If a person looks 'clean,' they can't have an STD." In fact, most people with an STD have no initial symptoms at all. Or, "I don't need to use a condom—I'm on the pill." In fact, birth-control methods such as the pill or Depo-Provera offer no STD protection. And, "my boyfriend/girlfriend loves me." Love and trust have nothing to do with it—most people with an STD don't even know they're infected.

Risk-taking, living for the moment and sexuality itself are normal aspects of adolescence, which can also place teens at risk for STDs. The long-term consequences of STDs seem remote, and are obscured by the more immediate wish to explore sex and experience intimacy. Normal adolescent insecurity over being liked and desired by peers can inhibit a teen from asking a partner to use a condom or from talking about STDs.

Sexy media messages often don't help. And "just say no" messages can have unintended consequences. Because many teens believe they're not supposed to be having sex, they don't carry a condom or plan ahead. But they may end up having unsafe sex when they are swept up in the moment.

Schools are an important partner in helping teens reduce STD risk—in fact, they are the primary source of STD information for most adolescents. Studies have found that classroom education can reduce sexual risk-taking in teens, and can be even more effective if supported by condom-availability programs and student health services. A recent evaluation of New York City's school condom-availability program showed that the program increased condom use among students at higher risk for STDs without increasing sexual activity overall. So far, three of the 52 L.A. County school districts with high schools have implemented condom-availability programs and school-based clinics.

Teens 15 to 19 have the highest rates of gonorrhea and chlamydia of any age group.

Seeking help for symptoms of an STD is often embarrassing for teens—just as it is for adults. In addition, many teens don't know where to go for STD testing, assume they can't afford it, or delay or forgo a clinic visit because they're afraid their parents will find out. Untreated STD infections can have potentially serious consequences even if initial symptoms are absent or have disappeared. Even without symptoms, teens can pass STDs to other sexual partners.

The health impact of STDs can be especially devastating for young people. Untreated chlamydia and gonorrhea infections, for example, can lead to infertility in those just entering their reproductive years. An HPV infection acquired by a 15-year-old girl, for example, can lead to cervical cancer by the time she's in her 30s. Painful herpes sores can recur for years or decades. Up to 10% of teens infected with hepatitis B will become chronic carriers, at increased risk of developing liver cancer and other complications.

Making the world a safer place

Sexually active teens should get tested for STDs at least once a year, or more often if they have new or multiple partners. Teens should know that by [California] state law they can receive STD testing and treatment without their parents' permission or knowledge, and that many clinics in L.A. County offer these services for free. The hepatitis B vaccine is also available free to eligible children and teens through the Vaccines for Children program.

No teen needs to suffer from an STD. Besides practicing safer sex and getting STD tests, teens should realize that putting off sexual involvement is a viable option: After all, in 12th grade, more than one-third of high school students have never had sex. But both teens and parents need to remember that there will come a time when children grow up and have sex for the first time. Will they know enough about STDs? Will they know how to use a condom? Will they be able to talk about these issues with a partner? By facing up to the facts about teen sexuality, we can make it a much safer world to grow up in.

5

Abstinence Is Increasing Among Young Teens

Vanessa Grigoriadis

Vanessa Grigoriadis is a freelance writer whose work has appeared in publications such as Spin, Cosmopolitan, New York Magazine, *and the* New York Times.

Organizations advocating sexual abstinence among teenagers have been gaining strength in the past decade, with the result that more teens are planning to retain their virginity longer. The organizations have focused on making abstinence seem cool, popular, and normal by targeting teen role models to promote their message. However, sex education programs that teach abstinence only are irresponsible because they fail to teach teens how to use contraception to protect themselves against sexually transmitted diseases and pregnancy if the teens should decide to break their abstinence pledge.

Arianne Keeler, 17, and Karen Sapp, 16, are high school juniors in the small, pristine city of Longmont, Colorado. For fun, they like to have sleepovers where they order pizza and play with Arianne's beagle. Their turn-ons include long walks in the mountains, singing, and renting movies. Their turn-offs are jocks, girls with swelled heads, and, unlike many of their post-pubescent classmates, premarital sex.

"Sex is tempting," admits Arianne, whose long blonde hair hangs loosely over a gray sweatshirt.

"Way tempting."

"It's a killer!" exclaims Karen, who wears a gold "purity ring" with the small silhouette of a dove on her wedding finger. "But then I think about how good it's going to feel on my wedding night. Oh!"

There's no school today because it's the day after Thanksgiving; the girls are eating lunch at a wood-paneled restaurant off a Colorado interstate with two guys, Adriel Fuentes and Arianne's boyfriend, Lonnie Hernandez, both of whom have also chosen to stay abstinent until marriage. "It's made us all a lot closer, for sure," says Adriel, a soft-spoken 17-year-old wearing a football jersey.

"It's the cool choice for everyone," says Karen.

"Like that girl Julie on *The Real World,*" adds Lonnie. "She was abstinent, and she was so cool."

"Or Jessica Simpson and her boyfriend, that guy from 98°," says Arianne, smiling widely. "They're virgins, too." ("That guy," Nick Lachey, may not be a virgin.)

"Right on," says Adriel. "Way to be."

But these kids weren't always so eager to be that way, least of all Arianne and Karen. In junior high, they would chase boys around at the mall and throw ice at them. On weekends, they told their parents they were going to the state fair but headed for the rodeo instead. The flannel shirts they wore at home covered up low-cut blouses and jeans so tight they say they had to lie down to zip them up. Once at the stadium, they hung out behind the chutes, with the cowboys—"We liked to check out the guys' butts," they say, laughing.

"Oh, I was a little slut," asserts Arianne, though she says petting was as far as she went. "But I always knew I wanted to wait until marriage, out of respect to myself and my future husband." (On her wrist she now wears a bracelet engraved with xoxo that Lonnie gave her—for hugs and kisses.) "I couldn't put on a white dress on my wedding day and have it be a lie."

Karen giggles, a hand flying up to cover her braces: "We still like checking out guys' butts, though."

Arianne and Karen aren't alone in their butt-checks-*good*, premarital-sex-*bad* mentality. Today, more teens plan to stay virgins longer than anytime in the last 20 years—statistics show the number of celibate males to be just shy of their female counterparts. According to the Centers for Disease Control and Prevention, 50 percent of high schoolers now graduate as virgins, up from 46 percent a decade ago. And while those four percentage points may not indicate the beginnings of a sex-free nation, they do represent the efforts of a highly orchestrated movement. Abstinence forces have been mobilizing for the last half decade, creating hundreds of organizations across the country that look to support the like-minded, convert the sinners, and—to the outrage of their myriad detractors—turn their point of view into law.

These de facto support groups tend to have cute acronyms such as STARS (Students Today Aren't Ready for Sex) or benign names like Operation Keepsake and Friends First, the Colorado-based group to which Arianne, Karen, Adriel, and Lonnie belong. Most advocate abstinence until marriage, though some add escape clauses upon high school graduation. Most are nonreligious—at least technically—attracting Christian youth leaders like Karen, sometime-churchgoers like Arianne, and kids like Adriel and Lonnie, who aren't religious. They make T-shirts with logos like VIRGIN POWER and bumper stickers that read PET YOUR DOG, NOT YOUR DATE; there's even an abstinence mascot, a green teddy bear endorsed by Miami Heat forward and vocal virgin A.C. Green.

"We've seen the sexual revolution come and go—and sex lost," says Leslee Unruh, the head of the world's largest chastity resource center, the National Abstinence Clearinghouse. "Now we're seeing the sexual *counter*-revolution."

In addition to offering foolproof ways to stave off the reaper, a nasty STD, or that tear-filled visit to Planned Parenthood, this supposed counter-revolution is reaching its target demographic by working on another major fear of adolescents: unpopularity. The groups are aggressive about making virginity seem not only normal but hip, promoting the stories of some of the youngest, most successful, and sexiest (but supposedly not sexually active) teen role models. So far, they've effectively linked their message to Britney Spears and her boyfriend, 'N Sync's Justin Timberlake; Jessica Simpson; and actress Leelee Sobieski—as well as tennis stars like the Williams sisters and Anna Kournikova. Reportedly having broken off her engagement to hockey star Pavel Bure, Kournikova maintains, "I'm still a virgin. I do not allow anyone to have a peep into my bed." Spears, too, is wont to proclaim her virginity (though the tabloids seem eager to prove otherwise): "If I have on a short skirt, it doesn't mean I have low morals," she's said. "There are so many young girls out there who are huge romantics and want to wait until they're married and believe in Prince Charming, like me."

But despite such ostensibly good intentions, pinning virgin badges to short skirts tends to rub some people the *wrong* way, especially in the case of teen teases like Spears (I *am* that innocent!). "Britney is a perfect example of the contradictory feelings people have about virgins," says Kennedy, MTV's original virgin VJ. "It's kind of lame to act slutty and not follow through. Plus, I'm really suspicious of virgins like that—it's just using virginity as another way to get your name in *In Style*."

Today, more teens plan to stay virgins longer than anytime in the last 20 years.

Spears and the like may be more concerned with image promotion than radical social change, but, in the process, they've provided the abstinence movement with a shiny, attractive package. Couple that with federally funded TV commercials extolling the pleasures of celibacy, myriad articles in teen magazines on the horrors of unwanted pregnancies and STDs, and the terrifying fact that 25 percent of new HIV cases in the U.S. are people younger than 22, and you have an environment where more and more teens are considering keeping it in their pants. And all this despite the average age of marriage reaching an all-time high of *27* and the increasingly sexualized nature of pop culture (duh)—from purring starlets like Lil' Kim and the casts of *Sex and the City* and MTV's *Undressed* to younger and younger models wearing less and less on the cover of every men's magazine. But do more sexually aggressive (role) models lead to more fans of sexual activity?

A *YM* poll of 15,000 teenage girls showed that 16 percent were having sex because of what they were seeing on TV; yet 76 percent also said television is where they learn about safe sex. Likewise from magazines, says Christina Ferrari, former managing editor of *Teen People*. "That's why we cover virginity and highlight celebrities talking about their virginity," she says. "Kids need role models who are willing to come out and say, 'I'm not having sex, and I'm not a loser or a geek,' because almost all kids have this completely false idea that everyone else is having sex." Clarifying *Teen People's* editorial mission, she adds, "At the same time, we're not out to say that sex is bad or that having sex is uncool."

Putting forth a similarly glossy though decidedly less open-minded ideology, abstinence groups like Friends First promote their message through colorful newsletters, classroom skits, websites, books, and videos that offer a blend of rhetoric about self-respect, daring to be different, and playing laser tag—which the Colorado branch recently did. ("I got MVP in my first game," brags Karen. "But then I shot you in the eyeball," says Lonnie.) Other perks of virginity include discounted tae kwon do lessons and 15 percent off at McDonald's. "And we had the most fun barbecue," says Arianne excitedly. "Afterwards, we played Truth or Dare. But we all took Truth."

She didn't get off that easily, though. Arianne was asked about a rumor that she'd given a boyfriend a blowjob—despite Clintonian logic, this does count as sexual relations. "I said no," says Arianne. "But everyone else in the game said, 'We know you did.'" And they were right. (While intercourse is down, experts are surmising from the dramatic increases in cases of oral herpes and gonorrhea in the upper throat that more and more teens are engaging in oral sex.)

The guy broke up with Arianne a week after the encounter. She worried that she might have contracted an STD, and immediately went for tests with Karen (the results were negative). She felt guilty about betraying not only her parents' wishes but her future husband as well. Soon, she found out that the guy had told a bunch of people at school. "A lot of the guys make these stupid motions with their mouths to tease me," she says, sitting cross-legged on her peach-colored comforter in her picture-perfect bedroom, the walls covered with posters of puppies and horses. "I'll never, ever make that mistake again."

Though the abstinence message has undergone some reconstructive surgery—losing some of its religion and its more graphic depictions of teen sex gone bad—its roots remain planted in the same conservative soil from which it sprang nearly 20 years ago in response to the free-loving '60s and '70s. The first group to make headlines as part of the new chastity movement was True Love Waits, a Christian youth organization made famous in 1994 for staking to the ground of the National Mall in Washington, D.C., more than 200,000 pastel-colored pledge cards from teens who swore to remain celibate until marriage. (To date, a million people have signed this pledge, including Jessica Simpson.) The act had symbolic meaning for the political right, which was then touting its social agenda with the Contract With America, a campaign against the perceived deterioration of "family values" (i.e., single moms, gay people, and graphic sex education in schools).

But the real victory for abstinence supporters came with the passage of the sweeping 1996 Welfare Reform Act, which included a provision about abstinence. Acting on the theory that less sex would translate into fewer indigent families and AIDS patients needing federal assistance, $50 million per year for five years was set aside for abstinence-only education under the bill's Title V. This education must stress, reads Title V, that sex before marriage is "likely to have harmful psychological and physical effects" and that abstinence from premarital sex is the "expected standard" for school-age children. This was to be taught in public schools from as early as fifth grade, and various methods of birth control were to be discussed only in terms of their failures (for example, that condoms can break, and that they don't protect effectively against all STDs, like human papilloma virus, which can result in cervical cancer in women).

"As sex ed became more than just plumbing class and the use of condoms was increasingly accepted to protect against AIDS, the religious movement really started to heat up," says Barbara Huberman of the progressive D.C. policy center Advocates for Youth. "The idea was that if you had good family values, you didn't have sex. It's absurd! What is immoral is not to give kids the tools, skills, and access to information about sexuality and protection so they can make their own choices."

"I sat in on an abstinence-only education class in a high school, and the woman who taught the class seemed more interested in inculcating discomfort than in informing [the kids] about their sexual choices," says Dan Savage, syndicated sex columnist and author. "At one point, she was having them call out all the possible consequences of sexual activity: 'You're going to get AIDS.' 'You're going to get pregnant.' 'You're going to die.' 'You're going to get date-raped.' And finally, I raised my hand, and I said, 'Pleasure, intimacy, contact.' She was dismissive."

[Given the] myriad articles in teen magazines on the horrors of unwanted pregnancies and STDs . . . you have an environment where more and more teens are considering keeping it in their pants.

Since the implementation of Title V in 1998, abstinence-only education has in fact been the only sex ed that 23 percent of American high schoolers receive. Though conservative supporters in Congress can expect much liberal opposition when the grant comes up for reauthorization this year, the program is widely respected on the right. During his campaign, President George W. Bush promised to add another $85 million to the budget, bringing the federal total to $135 million annually for abstinence-only education, versus roughly $30 million per year for "HIV education," a euphemism for sex ed. "It seems to me like the contraceptive message tends to undermine the message of abstinence," Bush has declared. "It sends a contradictory message."

Matt Smith, the spiky-haired Christian virgin from MTV's *The Real World: New Orleans,* who has become an eager spokesman for abstinence, agrees with President Bush. "Saying, 'Don't have sex, but here's the rubber, wink, wink'—that's a mixed message," he says. "And I don't believe in mixed messages." Essentially ignoring the 30 or so studies that show teaching safe sex in no way increases the likelihood of having sex, semi-celebrities like Smith and federally funded organizations like Friends First are successfully getting their unmixed messages to more and more kids who would normally never hear them.

Heavyset and handsome, Catholic by birth but not in practice, a Backstreet Boys fan who also has a Metallica tattoo on his bicep, Lonnie says he wouldn't have considered celibacy if it weren't for Friends First. He first came across the organization when members performed a skit at his junior high school (part of Friends First's mandate is to educate elementary and high school kids on sex, drugs, and alcohol, with the older students acting as mentors). He was drawn to the notion that abstinence would make him more mature—his dream is to become a singer/songwriter, but he plans to be a computer engineer in case it doesn't work out. When he got to high school, he, too, became a mentor to younger kids and has now become a Friends First "STAR," which stands for Self-Control, Trust, Abstinence, and Responsibility.

"For me, abstinence is more about achieving," says Lonnie. "Abstinence is the healthiest choice you can make as a person. I want to be the type of guy who takes full advantage of my skills and gifts, not someone who lets sex stand in the way."

That's all well and good, of course; who could argue with a person's quest to better himself? But how *responsible* is it to promote a message at the expense of the safety information that's needed should that message fail? A recent article in *The New York Times* reported that kids who took an abstinence pledge held out for 18 months longer than virgins who did not make a pledge. But it also showed that pledge-takers were less likely to use contraception during their first time—the probable result of not being educated about health risks and not planning for the encounter. Detractors like Huberman, Savage, and sex therapist and author Dr. Leonore Tiefer cite this as proof that abstinence-only education is a contradiction in terms. "Abstinence promoters are not interested in sex ed or providing information," says Tiefer. "Now it's, 'If you have sex, you'll be promiscuous and die of AIDS.' To them, better to be ignorant—then you'll be safe."

Whereas most abstinent male teens cite religion or the pursuit of career goals as reasons for remaining chaste, female virgins tend to be most motivated by the fear of becoming pregnant. While the teen pregnancy rate fell 17 percent in the last decade, the U.S. still leads industrialized nations in pregnancies among those younger than 19. Although we've made leaps and bounds from the "welfare mom" stereotype long bandied about by politicians, the fact is that poor black communities still have a separate set of problems than communities like Longmont, Colorado, when it comes to issues of teen sex.

"The people who most need the abstinence message are the African-American populations in the inner city," says Richard Panzer, a white, suburban 49-year-old dad of four and founder of Free Teens, a New Jersey-based abstinence group for teens, "because they're the most at risk."

Though it's as low as it's been in 40 years, the teen pregnancy rate of blacks is still currently twice that of whites. Free Teens, like many other small abstinence groups, produces educational videos and "relationship training" manuals and holds weekly exhortatory seminars at churches and community centers (boys and girls meet separately). They also sponsor all-night gatherings at bowling alleys or skating rinks, and the girls' group even had a sleepover at a Holiday Inn in Paterson, New Jersey, a midsize town where several bail-bond stores can be found on the same avenue. They rented six rooms for 30 girls, who stayed up all night playing cards and addressing each other by their Free Teens nicknames.

"That sleepover was so fun!" says Amber Dickson, a tall girl in a tie-dyed skirt. She's helping out at Free Teens' Thanksgiving luncheon for local seniors, a four-hour affair that features a step show and praise-dancing (*Star Search* moves set to gospel music). "Except I wanted pizza and they ordered chicken," continues Amber as she pours lemonade into beige plastic cups.

"And I was taking a shower when someone turned the lights off!" complains a tiny 15-year-old between bites of sweet potato pie.

"This one cleaned us all out at pinochle with her bag of nickels and a $20 bill none of us adults could break," laughs Yvonne Harvey, a pretty 27-year-old in a black leather jacket who often leads Free Teens meetings. Like many leaders in the abstinence movement, Harvey is a "born-again virgin," celibate for the last five years after becoming pregnant as a teen. (There are several groups out there for her, too, like the Seattle-based Born Again Virgins of America and the California-based Born Again Virgins, which organizes group trips with their club to exotic locales like Maui and the Virgin Islands.) "I just try to tell girls that it's not all about getting their freak on, blingity-bling-bling," says Harvey, swinging her leopard-print purse.

After the Thanksgiving luncheon, Yakeema Cobb, a tough, self-assured 15-year-old cheerleader in tight-fitting Pepe Jeans and a white T-shirt, heads back to the cramped ground-floor apartment where she lives with her mom, who had her when she was 17. "My mom doesn't want me to make the same mistakes she made," Yakeema says confidently. "And I'm not going to. I don't need a man to make me feel good about myself."

Kids need role models who are willing to come out and say, "I'm not having sex, and I'm not a loser or a geek."

Yakeema's room, essentially a glassed-in front porch, is small and neat and smells of the raspberry lotion she wears. She smiles mischievously. "You know, lots of guys like me . . . everywhere I go, someone is asking me out," she says, opening the top drawer of her pink bureau, in which there are dozens of little scraps of paper with scribbles on them. "I take all their numbers," she says, laughing, as she sifts through them. "But I don't call."

Though Yakeema immediately slips on a pair of Winnie the Pooh slippers upon entering her room and posters of Mickey Mouse hang on whatever wall space is available, a bunch of CDs are stacked next to her stereo: DMX, Lil' Kim, a single by Next. "I know I shouldn't be listening to that stuff," she says. "But, man, I just love that beat! I can't help myself."

Which raises the question: What happens when people simply can't help themselves when it comes to sex? The problem, of course, is that while true love may in fact wait, where sexual urges are concerned, a promise made is not always a promise kept. And in the case of the latter, the stakes are significantly higher.

"For any number of reasons, when you're in middle and high school years, you probably shouldn't be having sex—there's concern about STDs, pregnancy, hurt feelings, etc.," says Bill Albert, spokesperson for the National Campaign to Prevent Teen Pregnancy. "Sure, abstinence works—*if you're abstinent.* But at the end of the day, the only people who are getting pregnant or contracting diseases are those who aren't using contraception. I have yet to meet a teenager who finds that message confusing. It's the sexual equivalent of saying, 'You're too young to drink, but if you do, don't get behind the wheel of a car.'"

6

Teens Are Substituting Oral Sex for Intercourse

Bella English

Bella English is a staff writer for the Boston Globe.

Although surveys have found that fewer teens are having sexual intercourse, more are engaging in oral sex. Sex education classes emphasize the risks of intercourse but offer little information about alternative practices, such as oral sex. This leads many teens to believe that oral sex is a safe alternative to intercourse. As a result, many teens are engaging in oral sex at younger ages as a way to preserve their virginity.

The November [2000] dance at Weston [Massachusetts] Middle School was canceled. Not due to weather or lack of interest or chaperones. It was canceled because of dirty dancing. Or, to be specific, "inappropriate body contact" at the October dance.

To be very specific, a group of 20 to 25 kids were bumping and grinding to the music. Some boys removed their shirts. Some girls unbuttoned or unzipped the tops of their hip-huggers. The children involved were 12 and 13 years old.

"Dances are huge here, and it was hard to cancel it, but we needed to make a statement that the recreation department was not going to allow this kind of behavior," says Diane Dinell of the Weston Recreation Department, which sponsored the dance.

Not so long ago, at Catholic school dances, nuns would move from couple to couple, warning them to leave enough room "for the Holy Ghost." Today, you couldn't squeeze a toothpick between some of the young couples on the dance floor.

Sexual experimentation is beginning at a younger age

And "dirty dancing" may be the least of parental nightmares. Though there are few hard numbers on the sexual habits of young teens, the incident in Weston, Mass., and other anecdotal evidence suggests that they are becoming more sexually precocious. Nowadays, puberty begins at a younger age—and so, apparently, does sexual experimentation.

A "sin poll" conducted by a student newspaper at Milton (Mass.) Academy found 15 percent of freshmen reported having engaged in oral sex, twice the number who said they'd had intercourse. After a dirty dancing experience a few years ago, Collins Middle School in Salem, Mass., went into "shutdown," and the entire school developed rules for proper behavior at future dances. In a manuscript psychologist Michael Thompson just completed on children and social cruelty, he cites a survey in which 25 percent of eighth-graders reported fondling another's genitals.

"The big thing in the eighth and ninth grade used to be kissing and touching, and now that is being fast-forwarded to having oral sex," says Catherine Steiner-Adair, a Lexington, Mass., psychologist who treats adolescents and adults. Her message to both boys and girls is simple: Wait. "A bad early sexual experience can really affect you later on in having good, healthy romantic relations."

The good news is that there has been a decrease in sexual intercourse among teen-agers. According to a survey in 1999 by the Kaiser Family Foundation, slightly less than half of high school students had intercourse, down from 54 percent in 1991. But the other news is that more teen-agers are engaging in oral sex: 55 percent, the same survey found. They reason that they can't get pregnant and think—erroneously—that they can't get AIDS.

Slightly less than half of high school students had intercourse, down from 54 percent. . . . But the other news is that more teen-agers are engaging in oral sex: 55 percent.

Interviews reveal that many middle schoolers are following the high schoolers' lead. "People are pretty wary about having real sex," says one 13-year-old boy at a suburban school where an eighth-grade girl was recently discovered performing oral sex on a male classmate. With intercourse, he says, "a lot can go wrong. It can screw up your life." But the boy and his friends don't equate oral sex with actually having sex. "It's just hooking up," he says. "It happens all the time."

And dirty dancing? "It's not like a sexy thing," says 14-year-old George Sholley of Milton. "It's just the way you dance."

In today's teen lingo, "hooking up" is the term of choice, and it can mean "anything from kissing to third base; it's not the home run," as the 13-year-old boy puts it.

Stacey Harris, a 12-year-old who attends Milton Academy, has seen couples making out at parties since early sixth grade. "There is peer pressure to hook up. You gotta know that just because you don't, people won't hate you," she says. "The guys who hook up are cool, but the girls are called sluts or ho's. There's no such thing as a guy slut."

Therapists who treat adolescents are hearing more and more from girls who feel coerced into substituting oral sex for intercourse. And in interviews, middle school girls describe oral sex as a way of preserving their virginity.

"It's totally different from real sex," says one 14-year-old who attends a private girls' school. "We don't call it sex. It's very common in the eighth grade. Girls do it to be cool, and to protect their reputations." It's OK to have oral sex at her age or younger, she says, but not sexual intercourse. "The worst thing that can happen to a girl is to get pregnant."

Two eighth-grade girls who attend a Dorchester middle school in Boston say that pressure from boys to perform oral sex starts in the seventh grade. "Boys will say, 'Will you do me?' I say, 'No way.' It's not worth the diseases," says one 13-year-old.

Therapists who treat adolescents are hearing more and more from girls who feel coerced into substituting oral sex for intercourse.

Talk to the boys, however, and they deny any coercion. "We ask them, and if they say no, that's their choice," says one 14-year-old boy. He adds: "But sooner or later, they may say yes." His two friends nod in agreement.

Thompson, who has written several books on adolescents, tells of a seventh-grade boy who engaged in oral sex with an eighth-grade girl. "He said to me, 'I know this is supposed to be very exciting, but I haven't reached puberty yet.'"

Generally, though, it's the other way around: The boy is the instigator. Many girls see oral sex as a bargain, says Deborah Roffman, a health educator whose book, *Sex and Sensibility: The Thinking Parents' Guide to Talking Sense About Sex,* is due out in January.

"They think, 'He'll stop pressuring me to have intercourse if I do this.' The girls also think it puts them in control. But it's a no-win situation for them. It's just a cutting of their losses," she says. "This kind of early sexual behavior is sexist and dehumanizing, and the girls don't even get it."

A visible minority

Experts stress that it is still the minority of young teens who are actually having some sort of sexual experience. "The majority are intensely interested in what's going on," says Thompson, who is also the counselor at the Belmont Hill School in Belmont, Mass. "But they're holding back, seeing what the impact is."

But—as was the case in Weston—the involved minority is a very visible minority: the popular kids. "It's the kids who want to be the social leaders, who want to set the pace, and they're going to take the risks to dazzle everybody else," says Thompson. "The majority can stand back and watch and talk a lot about it and sort of get off vicariously on what they're doing."

Parents shocked by reports of such behavior so early need to take a close look at the messages they are sending their kids, experts say. Allowing unlimited access to the Internet or MTV and letting R-rated movies regularly into the home all desensitize children to the issue of sex. Then there's the time-honored parental emphasis on intercourse and pregnancy when talking about sex.

"We parents have persistently said that the only kind of real sex is intercourse, and we reinforce the notion that the rest of it is not real; it doesn't have consequences," Roffman says. "The parents are not there. They are not giving the kids the right information, clear values and clear limits. So kids are free to experiment with things based on their very limited view, which they get from TV and each other."

One result, says Erika Guy, assistant headmaster at the Noble and Greenough School in Dedham, Mass., is that oral sex has become the sexual issue that "more than anything else divides our generations." Students are astounded to hear her label it "the most intimate act," and she, in turn, is astounded at their more casual attitude.

"I was saying that this is the far reaches of intimate sex, and they were saying that this was entry-level sex," she says. "There's a real generational split here. To them, it's OK."

A sexualized culture

A major culprit seems to be the highly sexualized popular culture—preaching abstinence to teens yet targeting them with suggestive lyrics, commercials and movies—from which young people take their cues. "If kids are seeing and hearing about how prevalent sex is in the lives of celebrities, then they want to experience that for themselves," says 14-year-old Sholley.

From MTV to Abercrombie and Fitch ads, males with their hands on their crotches are prevalent, surrounded by girls in suggestive clothing and positions. Britney Spears does a striptease at the MTV Awards, and hard-core pornography pervades the Internet. The number of sexual references on mainstream TV tripled during the 1990s, according to the Parents Television Council.

And music is eroding the taboo against oral sex among black youths. "Rappers have put it out there, and now it's considered popular among the kids," says Matt Balls, director of teen services at the Roxbury Boys and Girls Club.

Just turn on MTV, Guy advises parents. "Eighty percent of the dance movements really mimic a sexual act," she says. "Look at the advertising in magazines. The kids are swimming in all of this, and parents don't even realize it."

And the targets are increasingly becoming younger and younger children.

Oral sex has become the sexual issue that "more than anything else divides our generations."

"Through no fault of their own," says Steiner-Adair, "the popular culture is unusually sexually violent, demeaning, and cynical about love and tenderness and heartfelt connections between men and women."

Kathleen Hassan, who leads a self-esteem group for girls ages 11 to 14 in Milton, Mass., called Girls' Voices/Good Choices, was surprised when she asked her 4-year-old niece to sing her a song. "I expected 'The Itsy

Bitsy Spider,'" she says, "but she started singing, 'Oops! . . . I Did It Again' by Britney Spears," with the refrain, "I'm not that innocent."

If children are not that innocent these days, they need to hear more from the adults in their lives, experts say. "My daughter and I talk about it all," says the mother of the ninth-grader who attends the all-girls' school. "I know some of her friends are into this. I feel with all the pressure out there, my voice needs to be louder."

Dirty dancing

A few years ago, when students at Collins Middle School in Salem were dirty dancing and adults intervened, principal Mary Manning canceled classes so that students and faculty could discuss it. "It was pretty intense," says Manning. Students came up with six rules for school dances, including no grinding or dirty dancing; dance with both feet on the floor ("as opposed to one wrapped around someone or something," says Manning) and no sandwich dancing.

Sandwich dancing? "Do you really want to know?" chuckles Manning. "It's when one person is very close behind you and one person is very close facing you, and, well, let your imagination take over."

Most parents, says Thompson, start discussions two years too late; frank talk should begin at least by age 10. "Puberty's coming earlier and earlier and earlier," he says, "and then we're astonished when they take these bodies out and flash them around."

Laura Jenks-Daly, a Weston mother of three, says her 16- and 19-year-old daughters were appalled when they heard about the dirty dancing at the town's dance from their 12-year-old sister, who witnessed the behavior. "Things are just starting younger and younger, and they don't have anything to compare it to, except what they see on TV," she says.

Another Weston mother, Tricia Scarpato, has encountered parents who are in denial about what goes on: "I've had some very bad experiences calling parents," she says. "They say, 'Oh, that's not my child,' or 'How dare you?' When I was a kid and I did something wrong, somebody's parent or a neighbor would tell, and by the time I got home, my parents already knew about it. Today, parents are reluctant to talk to each other, but we have to."

Roffman sees sexualized middle schoolers as both a symptom of lost values and a wake-up call to parents.

"This is about body parts relating to body parts, not about human beings engaged in intimate behavior," she says. "These kids are going to be jaded. If you've done oral sex in the eighth grade, what's next? These kids have totally missed out on the idea of sex as intimacy.

"We adults have to understand that we are raising kids in the world as it is and not as we want it to be," she adds. "We have to stop looking at the world through our eyes and see the world through their eyes."

7

Teens Are Becoming Sexually Experienced at Younger Ages

Anne Jarrell

Anne Jarrell is a former copy editor for the New York Times *and reporter/feature writer for the* Chicago-Sun Times. *Her work has appeared in the* North Atlantic Review.

A significant number of children are engaging in sexual activities before they even reach their teenage years. By the time they are teenagers, many of them will have had intercourse. Accompanying the sexual precociousness is a casual and brazen attitude toward sex. Many psychiatrists and psychologists are concerned about the health and emotional ramifications for these adolescents. They maintain that schools should provide not only sex education in earlier grades but forums where youngsters can explore their feelings and discuss the sexual messages promoted in popular culture.

On the Upper West Side of New York City, Dr. Marsha Levy-Warren, a psychologist, said she is seeing more and more preteenagers who are going on junior versions of dates in fifth grade, at 10 or 11 years old. By seventh grade, they have graduated to sex.

"I can't tell you how many girls come in who are bereft about having had sex too soon," she said. "They went to a party, met a cute guy, he seemed to like them, they hooked up and did what they assumed everyone was doing. Then, they feel awful."

On the Upper East Side, Dr. Cynthia Pegler, a specialist in adolescent medicine, sees girls brought in by their mothers when they outgrow the pediatrician. These sophisticated young women may not be having intercourse at 13, but they are having oral sex. "They tell me oral sex is no big deal," Dr. Pegler said. "They don't see it as sex, but as safe and fun and a prelude to intercourse, where before, it used to be the other way around."

And in the suburbs, on Long Island, Dr. Wayne Warren, a psychologist, said groups of seventh and eighth graders rent limousines to take them to clubs in Manhattan, where they get drunk, grind on the dance floor and have oral sex in dim corners.

Sex at younger and younger ages

In a society that is always pushing the envelope, the age at which sexual experimentation begins is speeding up, too, say psychotherapists, health professionals and school officials, who are concerned about the health and emotional ramifications for young teenagers.

"There are significant numbers of youngsters who are engaging in sexual activity at earlier ages," said Dr. Robert W. Blum, a physician and the director of the division of general pediatrics and adolescent health at the University of Minnesota, which analyzes data on teenage sexual activity for the federal government. "Besides intercourse, they are engaging in oral sex, mutual masturbation, nudity and exposure as precursors to intercourse."

In data published by Dr. Blum and his team in the *Journal of the American Medical Association* in 1997, 17 percent of a national sample of thousands of seventh and eighth graders had had intercourse. Other, smaller studies put the percentage even higher.

"I see no reason not to believe that soon a substantial number of youths will be having intercourse in the middle-school years," said Dr. Richard Gallagher, director of the Parenting Institute at New York University's Child Study Center. "It's already happening."

Many reasons

Experts of all political and philosophical bents give many reasons for this phenomenon, including the rising divorce rate, inattentive parents, the availability of condoms and the earlier onset of puberty. But the most frequent explanation is that today's culture sends a very mixed message to its young.

On the one hand, bombarded by warnings about AIDS and sexually transmitted diseases, adolescents are taught abstinence, the sole contraception method taught at one-third of all public schools across the country, according to a poll by the Alan Guttmacher Institute, a private research organization.

More and more preteenagers . . . are going on junior versions of dates in fifth grade, at 10 or 11 years old. By seventh grade, they have graduated to sex.

On the other hand, teenagers are confronted daily with a culture that has become a very sexy place indeed in which to live. "Sex is everywhere, and it's absolutely explicit," said Dr. Allen Waltzman, a psychiatrist with practices on the Upper East Side and in Brooklyn, who sees many adolescents. "There's hardly a film that doesn't show a man and a woman having sex. There's MTV, lurid rap lyrics, and now we've got techno-sex on the Internet."

None of this is lost on young adolescents, Dr. Waltzman said. "Kids always push to the limit of what's permitted in a society."

One 13-year-old boy at a junior high school in Manhattan said he first had oral sex at 12 and has had it about eight times at parties and in the hours between 4 p.m. and 7, before parents come home from work. The sex was never with a steady girlfriend, because he has never had one. "It's something to do with someone," he said. "I think it's curiosity. I don't think that's bad."

An eighth-grade private-school boy said that he and his friends know that oral sex "is not perfect," but that they believe there is less likelihood of picking up a sexually transmitted disease than with intercourse. "The schools tell us to refrain, they tell you you get S.T.D.'s from both, but no one believes it," he said.

Dr. Warren, who practices in Manhattan as well as in Suffolk County, said: "Before, the dialogue was, 'I love you and care for you, so let's experiment.' Now, the dialogue is, 'This is safe and fun and O.K., and you have nothing to worry about.'

"I see girls, seventh and eighth graders, even sixth graders, who tell me they're virgins, and they're going to wait to have intercourse until they meet the man they'll marry. But then they've had oral sex 50 or 60 times. It's like a goodnight kiss to them, how they say goodbye after a date."

What the studies show

There are no in-depth studies showing national trends in sexual activity in middle school, ages 10 to 13. No one will finance such studies, Dr. Blum said, because of fear of the outcry from politicians who embrace an abstinence-only message and from parents wanting to protect their children's privacy.

The studies of national trends that do exist look only at high school students. These show a striking drop decade by decade in the age at which teenagers first engage in intercourse. A December 1999 study by the National Center on Addiction and Substance Abuse at Columbia University noted that in the early 1970's, less than 5 percent of 15-year-old girls and 20 percent of 15-year-old boys had engaged in sexual intercourse. By 1997, the figures were 38 percent for girls, 45 percent for boys.

In the wake of AIDS and of abstinence advocacy, statistics from the 1990's analyzed by the Guttmacher Institute show that the age by which a majority of teenagers had engaged in intercourse has not continued to fall. The teenage birthrate has been falling since 1991, in part, experts say, because of decreased sexual activity. (It is still the highest for the developed world.) The Centers for Disease Control and Prevention in Atlanta reports that among high school students of all ages, those who have had sex declined from 53 percent in 1995 to 48.4 percent in 1997, the latest year for which figures are available.

But Dr. Gallagher said that the apparent diminishing of high school sexual activity masks a more insidious development: some older teenagers may be extending their years of virginity, but some younger teenagers are having sex earlier.

"You can get 16- to 18-year-olds who will be very conservative sexually," Dr. Gallagher said. "And then you can get right below them a group of 14- to 16-year-olds who say those older students are too conservative, let's party."

Despite the paucity of data about young teenagers, educators say that the anecdotal evidence points to increased sexual activity, often of a detached, unemotional kind.

"The kids are overwhelmed with sexual messages, and we're seeing a younger and younger display of not only precocious sexual behavior but also aggressive sexual molestation, like holding down a student and forcibly pulling down his or her pants," said Dr. Frederick Kaeser, the director of health services for District 2 of the New York public school system, covering much of Manhattan.

"We do a terrible job of teaching sex education," he added.

A typical timetable

One boy, 13, who attends a private school in Manhattan, said his interest in sex began in the third grade, watching *Beverly Hills 90210,* the television show that portrayed teenagers from well-off families in the boom economy behaving like adults. "I was interested," he said. "The people were cool. I wanted to try what they were doing on the show."

He, along with half a dozen of his friends, described a timetable for sexual initiation. By third grade, they knew the slang for activities from masturbation to oral sex. By fourth grade, they had girlfriends and were playing kissing games. By fifth, they were going on dates. In sixth, they were French kissing and petting. In seventh and eighth grades, they tried oral sex, and some had intercourse.

By ninth grade, one boy said, "it's just one big spree of going all the way."

The head of their school said she thought they were accurate in their timetable.

Asked if they felt things were going too fast, the boys shrugged. "It has to happen sooner or later," the 13-year-old said. "Sex is pleasurable. Why not now? Sometimes people get hurt. Sure. I've been hurt. But that's going to happen at any age."

Psychiatrists and psychologists, however, say that most young teenagers cannot handle the profound feelings that go with early sex. "Developmentally, they just aren't ready," Dr. Levy-Warren said. "They're trying to figure out who they are, and unlike adults who obsess first and then act, kids do the opposite—they act and then obsess. They jump into this, and are left with intense feelings they're unable to sort out."

What's most troubling to Dr. Levy-Warren and others is a new casual, brazen attitude about sex. "I call it body-part sex," she said. "The kids don't even look at each other. It's mechanical, dehumanizing. The fallout is that later in life they have trouble forming relationships. They're jaded."

No clear answers

While New York middle-school educators and counselors say they are increasingly concerned about earlier sexual activity, particularly oral sex, no one is clear on what to do about it. After Schools Chancellor Joseph A. Fernandez was fired in 1993, in part for introducing a condom-distribution program, the New York public schools have settled into a sex education curriculum that's a mixed bag of preaching, basic anatomy and, in high school, condom distribution, though parents can choose to keep their children from participating.

Even at New York's private schools, not concerned with federal guidelines, which since 1996 have allocated millions of dollars to sex education programs that teach only abstinence, ambivalence reigns. At Friends Seminary in downtown Manhattan, parents were called to a meeting two years ago after students in a fifth grade class began pairing off and breaking up, and "the misery factor was high," said Pamela Wood, the head of the middle school. There was no consensus among the adults. Half were appalled at the prospect of 10-year-olds dating. The other half thought it was cute.

"In elementary school, everyone pretty much has the same agenda," Ms. Wood said. "By middle school, no one agrees on what is appropriate. As for parents, their egos can get entangled. They want their kids to be liked, and if dating is what it requires, then they're for it."

The sex education curriculum at Friends includes practice exercises in how to put on a condom for eighth graders and free condom distribution in high school, but there is disagreement about distributing condoms with fruit flavoring, for use during oral sex.

At the Dalton School on the Upper East Side, concern about the precocious sexual climate led to starting a sex education program for the fifth grade, where none had existed so early before.

I see girls, seventh and eighth graders, even sixth graders, who tell me they're virgins. . . . But . . . they've had oral sex 50 or 60 times. It's like a goodnight kiss to them.

Dr. Glenn Stein, the middle-school psychologist, said that the program is mostly anatomy. "A little inoculation, I would call it," he said. "It's not enough, but it's a start."

What the fast-sex scene means to girls, as opposed to boys, is of particular concern to school psychologists, who mentioned holding discussions and seminars on gender issues. Deborah Tolman, a director at the Wellesley College Center for Research on Women, points out that anecdotal evidence indicates that when it comes to oral sex, "the boys are getting it, the girls no."

"It's the heterosexual script that entitles boys and disables girls," she said.

Most psychologists say that what is needed is not just to supply youngsters with facts and information about anatomy, but also to provide them with forums to explore their feelings and to digest the proliferation of sexual messages they receive. As Francesca Schwartz, a school psychologist at the Brearley School, a private school for girls on the Upper East Side, put it: "Do I really like this person? Or am I just doing this to be popular? These are the questions the kids need to learn to think about and ask."

Such discussions should come sooner rather than later, educators say. "Preteens in our culture are 8 and 9," said Dr. Ava L. Siegler, a psychologist and the author of "The Essential Guide to the New Adolescence." "We shouldn't wait to talk to them about AIDS, sex and violence until they are 12."

Dr. Waltzman added: "To kids, their crushes and loves are the most important thing. Adults may see it as silly or irrelevant, but the kids don't. It does no good to leave them to figure it out on their own."

8

Sexual Activity Among Adolescent Girls Is Increasing

Liza Mundy

Liza Mundy is a staff writer for the Washington Post Magazine.

American popular culture is filled with sexual references, innuendo, and images that teens are readily and eagerly absorbing. As a result, today's young girls are becoming sexually aware—and active—at an unprecedented rate. For many girls, their sexual experimentation is a result of pressure and coercion by boys—both in their own age group and older. While some girls actively pursue these sexual encounters, the strong double standard that condemns girls but not boys for being sexually active generally means that girls are not using sex to empower themselves. In addition, the use by educators of scare tactics to discourage teen sex have perhaps led to the phenomenon in which boys target younger and younger girls in order to avoid catching sexually transmitted diseases.

Morning brings the invitations. The casual ones. So routine are they that she hardly thinks about them, just waves them away like gnats. Today, for example, a boy came up to her in the hall and asked, "When are you going to let me hit that?" "That means, like, intercourse," the girl explains, with a sort of gum-popping matter-of-factness. She is 13.

She is an eighth-grader, fresh-faced, clear-eyed, with light brown hair and fluffy bangs and plucked eyebrows, her voice sweet and straightforward as, one morning in an unused classroom, she sits relating some of the other things guys say to her in the halls of her Montgomery County [Maryland] middle school, nestled in developed farmland in the central part of the county.

"They say, 'What's up with the dome?'" the girl continues, explaining that this is an invitation to perform oral sex, as is the more familiar: "When are you going to give me head?" She tells them never. She laughs. Whatever it takes to put them off. She has not done much more than kiss, though she and her female friends talk about sex a lot, especially oral sex. "They're like, 'It's not that bad once you do it. But it's scary the first time.'

I guess they're nervous that they won't do it right. They said they didn't have any pleasure in it. They did it to make the boys happy, I guess."

She thinks that someday she will do it.

She thinks that it will be gross.

The serious invitations come in the afternoon, after school, from two boys she knows well, boys who live within walking distance of her house, boys who call her up, or else she calls them, and they come over when her parents are still at work and the only other person in her house is a sibling. When the boys arrive they often say something like what one of them said just the other day: "Let's go to your room. You can give me some head and then we'll go downstairs." To which she replied: "No! You're nasty!"

For all the recent decline in teen pregnancies and abortions, there is nevertheless more sexual activity *at every stage of adolescence now than there was 30 years ago.*

It is a little complicated to explain who the two boys are. One of them—let's call him Boy A—used to be her boyfriend and is now just her friend. The two of them talk a lot—they're really close, they know each other's life story, he has told her everything about himself and his past, though she's not sure she believes all of it (how much past can an eighth-grader have?), and they've had conversations about oral sex. For example, the one in which she said to him, "If I do it to you and do it wrong, just tell me what I'm doing wrong so I can fix it."

The invitations also come from Boy B. One day, for example, back when she was going out with Boy A, she and Boy B were talking on the phone in the afternoon, and she invited the two of them over, and Boy B "was, like, 'Are you going to give him head?' And I was, like, 'No.' And then he asked about himself—he was, like, 'What about me?' And I was, like, 'No.' I was, like, 'Heck no!' and he was, like, 'Why?' And I was, like, 'Because I don't like you,' and he was, like, 'So? You can still do it!'"

"They always ask," she says. "Even if you say no 700 times, they'll always ask you."

What if the boys were to suddenly leave her alone and stop asking? "I would think they didn't like me or something," she says, "or that the other girls are prettier or, like, better than me."

What if she gives in? Just goes ahead and gets it over with? She has thought about this. For example, she knows that if she did it with Boy A, Boy A would tell Boy B, and likewise, if she did it with Boy B, Boy B would tell Boy A. So people would know. She doesn't think it would affect her reputation; you only get a bad reputation if you have sex with every boy who asks you. But the one thing she knows is that if she did it, even once, and people found out, her day would be one endless stream of requests. "They would ask me, and ask me, even more than they do now."

In other words, this girl—who asked, for obvious reasons, that her name not be used in this article—is making complex moral calculations all day long, measuring popularity, fending off unwanted commentary, admitting to curiosity, assessing risk. At least until her mother gets home. "How was your day at school?" she usually asks.

A safe time to come of age?

Statistically, you might think that this is a relatively good—or at least, a relatively safe—time to be coming of age, sexually, in America. The important numbers—as reported by the Alan Guttmacher Institute, the National Center for Health Statistics and other research groups—show:

Teen pregnancy rate, down 16 percent between 1991 and 1996.

Teen abortion rate, down 22 percent in the same period.

Teen birth rate, down 18 percent.

Contraceptive use way up since 1979, when fewer than half of adolescents used contraception the first time they had sex. Now, more than 70 percent do, though less than half say they use contraception every time.

All of these trends, found in every state, every region of the country.

A relatively safe time to be coming of age.

Except: What should we think about a brown-haired girl in a classroom struggling to think of some boys who *don't* ask her for sex? "The only friends I know who don't do it," she says "are, like, friends I've known since—well, two or three friends don't do it."

What should we think about similar conversations with other young teens around Montgomery County; an eighth-grader, for example, who kept a diary at my request documenting the stream of unwanted sexual come-ons she fends off every day? One entry, written in careful cursive in light blue ink on notebook paper, read: "I was bending down, getting something from out of my locker when a boy just came up behind and was trying to hump me." Another: "I was at my locker picking up my books from off the floor and a boy stands in front of me and puts his [crotch] in my face and says, 'Oh yes, you're the best.'"

What should we think about five Bethesda [Maryland] eighth-graders standing at a picnic, saying that each of them knows a classmate who has had sex? "My mom doesn't know this goes on," says one. "She thinks we don't even kiss. I don't tell my parents anything. I don't want to tell them. They wouldn't understand. They'd think I was retarded."

As an eighth-grader myself, I can recall being exposed to very little sexual imagery, aside from the relatively subtle innuendo of rock lyrics.

What should we think about statistics showing that, for all the recent decline in teen pregnancies and abortions, there is nevertheless more sexual *activity* at every stage of adolescence now than there was 30 years ago? About the fact that, over the same time period, the average age of first sexual intercourse has dropped by a full year (from 18 to 17 for girls, from 17 to 16 for boys)? About research showing that one-fifth of all 15-year-olds have had sex at least once?

What should we think about the fact that—even as the overall percentage of sexually active teens has declined slightly during the past couple of years—for girls under 15 it has continued to increase?

"Our culture is to a large extent experimenting with eroticizing the child," says David Murray, an anthropologist and research director at the Statistical Assessment Service, a think tank in Washington. Look, Murray suggests, at the cult of Britney Spears, or the continued newsstand appeal of the murdered 6-year-old JonBenet Ramsey. What's going on, Murray says, is not a healthy expression of our culture's sensuality through a fond depiction of the female form. It's not some hip literary Lolita thing, not a fundamentally harmless Alice in Wonderland-type doting uncle thing. It's not a Maurice Chevalier love-those-bows-and-ruffles thing. It's not innocent. It's not affectionate. It's base. It's weird. It's commerce.

"It's the *commodification* of the eroticization of the child," Murray adds. "We celebrate it."

A different time

I've long wondered about this. That is, I've wondered what it must be like, for girls, and for boys, too, to be coming of age in an era shaped by both the '60s sexual revolution and the '80s AIDS onslaught; coming of age in the time of *Dawson's Creek* and *Sex and the City;* a time of HIV and Eminem; a time when Lorena and John Bobbitt and Monica Lewinsky and Bill Clinton have done more than anybody else to insinuate terms like "penis" and "oral sex" into family newspapers like this one. A time when the media—all media, even mainstream media—are more sexualized than they've ever been, and yet, at the same time, the consequences of sex are depicted so grimly, by cultural conservatives and liberals alike. What does it feel like—how does a kid respond—when the messages are so mixed and so insistent?

Sex is great!

Sex can be fatal!

"What do you worry more about: sex on television or violence on television?" I asked a man at a party about four years ago. Like most parents at most parties, we were eating buffet food and talking about our kids. The father of three sons, he replied that violence was what he worried about; his sons liked violent TV, they liked action movies and video games, and all of this, he felt, had coarsened his boys' character. Sex on the screen was not something he'd given much thought to.

I felt precisely the opposite.

Twenty-five years ago, as an eighth-grader myself, I can recall being exposed to very little sexual imagery, aside from the relatively subtle innuendo of rock lyrics. Apart from that, I remember few explicit sexual references in the broad popular culture, and even those weren't really popular culture per se. For example, I remember sometime in my early teens when my parents took me to *Walkabout,* an Australian movie where there is a brief shot of full frontal female nudity, or the time my friend Kate and I, for reasons that still elude me, went to see Fellini's *Amarcord,* of which I remember (of course) only the boy's face smashed in the fat woman's breasts. Instances like these were so infrequent, and so memorable, that I can count them on my fingers. The rest of the time, I was watching Arte Johnson fall off a tricycle on *Laugh-In.*

Now, it seems as if each new day pushes the edge of the envelope further. Just last week I was sitting on the couch with my daughter, now 4½, and the TV was tuned to my favorite show, the British series *Absolutely Fabulous*, on Comedy Central. During one break there was a teaser for a routine that would be aired later that night. In it, a comic was saying: "Bush-Gore, Bush-Gore: What kind of a presidential contest is that? It sounds more like a snuff movie!" Fortunately the reference went over my daughter's head, but what, I couldn't help but wonder, if it hadn't? I didn't learn what a snuff movie was until I was 30, and only then because I'm married to the son of a cop, who used to confiscate them. What if my daughter had been slightly older—6, say—and asked me what a snuff movie is? What if my son, now 2, was also sitting there? What would I tell them?

For some parents, of course, the solution is to not get cable: That way your kids can't watch Comedy Central, or MTV movies like *Jailbait*, or Dr. Drew's sex advice show, though they still could watch *Friends*, or *Buffy*, or *Fresh Prince*, or many of the other TV shows showing relationship-obsessed young people. Or they might go on the Internet, as I did recently, and type in the search terms "teen" and "sex," whereupon they will be rewarded with a zillion links to pornography sites such as WORLD TEEN SEX ("20 Tiny Lolitas!") and SUKEBE 500 FROM JAPAN ("cute school girl from Tokyo") and TEEN SEX, HARDCORE SEX AND FREE PORN WITH TEEN ("amateurs and young girls having sex") and SEXY TEEN GIRL ("Sex pictures gallery! Cleanest looking teens!").

There are filtering devices, of course, but there is also ordinary old FM radio, which I was listening to recently while driving with my kids. Between music segments, a commercial came on that went: "Sex with a regular condom is like this"—noise of a dripping faucet—"but sex with our supercharged ribbed condom is like THIS"—noise of a roaring waterfall!!

I'm not saying that all of this is bad. Temperamentally I'm always inclined to think that information is a good thing; that sexual awareness is a good thing. In particular, it has always bothered me that our culture and literature contain so few explorations of adolescent female desire; that there's no girl's version of *Portnoy's Complaint*. I know many women who regard their own sexual initiation as a fun and hilarious time, a time they will remember fondly when they are old women in rocking chairs thinking back on their lives.

But how—in this era—to regulate the flow of information? What to do when there is no childhood terrain that's sacrosanct? The other day I was at my local playground, and looked down to see that my daughter had unknowingly dug up a used condom in a scoopful of sand. What did she think when she saw grown-ups dashing about, trying to find a napkin or paper towel to pick up the condom, and surreptitiously assessing—even as we knew we were overreacting—the statistical odds of HIV contamination?

An eighth-grade sex-ed class

"How many of you are sexually active?" Aury Coronado asked a group of girls who were slouched in chairs, gazing out the window, contemplating their nails and, in one case, it appeared, napping. Aury is a nurse and a health educator, and on this particular day she was in a comfortable room at a Kensington medical office, conducting an after-school contraception class for a group of Montgomery County eighth-graders. There were nine girls in the room, and none raised a hand. The counselor who'd brought them from their school looked amused. She knew they were just leery about unburdening themselves to a stranger. "How many of you are *sexually active?*" the counselor repeated.

"Do you mean, *do* we or *have* we?" one of the girls said.

"Have you," she said, whereupon the girls snapped to, and six of them raised their hands.

Little research has been done on teenagers under 15, partly because for a long time, researchers didn't think this age group was relevant.

I learned later that this group of eighth-graders was somewhat unusual; the term for them once upon a time might have been fast girls, though I would discover that there was a great deal of heterogeneity in the group; some of the girls strongly disapproved of what others were doing. A better word now might be "at risk," which is to say that many of them were girls from low-income, single-parent or otherwise disadvantaged households. But even given their very specific demographic, it struck me as remarkable that six out of nine of them had had sex, at 13 or 14. What also struck me, as I listened to Aury's very useful discourse with them, was the mix of experience and ignorance they displayed. Their first question, which they'd written down in advance, was what is a female condom, and when Aury told them that the female condom isn't very appealing to look at, that it sort of hangs outside the woman's body, there was a smirk and one of the girls said knowingly, "It doesn't look very appetizing!"

On one level they were very worldly and on another they were full of superstition and childlike curiosity. When they'd come to trust Aury they asked her all sorts of questions, like whether it is true that you can get pubic lice in your armpits and eyebrows, and whether you can get pregnant from oral sex, and whether plastic wrap is an acceptable means of protection from sexually transmitted diseases, and whether one ought to douche, and if so whether one ought to douche with vinegar (no, no, no, no, and no). Another thing they wanted to know was whether people over 50 are allowed to have sex, and if so, whether this is really a good idea.

"I thought there was, like, an age to stop," one of them said. "'Cuz, you know, some of them get home and have heart attacks." When Aury told the group that even people in nursing homes have sex, the girls fell silent with shock.

Afterward, I kept thinking about this session, about what these young girls knew and didn't know and had done and were doing. Were they exceptions? In the level of their experience, probably. Clearly there are children who spend most of middle school thinking about sports, and friends, and music, and, I don't know, the cafeteria menu. But there are lots and lots of middle-schoolers whose experience of life, and sex, falls somewhere between inactivity and immersion. Exactly where is something that people in the field find it difficult to agree on: Little research has been done on teenagers under 15, partly because for a long time, researchers didn't think this age group was relevant to social problems like teen pregnancy and sexually transmitted diseases, and also because it wasn't considered seemly to ask.

In particular, there is controversy over whether it's true—as has been reported—that there is a lot more oral sex now among middle-schoolers. There are no statistics on this yet, but based on experience and anecdote, many front-liners in the field are convinced that this is true. "When I was growing up, you didn't hear a lot about oral sex, especially in middle school," says Krystal Holland-McKinney, a sexuality counselor who works extensively with kids in Maryland, the District of Columbia and Virginia. "Now it's happening in middle school and it's happening cross-culturally."

In turn, people like Michael Resnick, director of the National Teen Pregnancy Prevention Research Center, say, "This is nothing new." Resnick isn't debating whether teenagers are having oral sex; he's simply arguing that teenagers have been having oral sex for quite some time, that they began well before the great media pile-on that began with President Clinton's indiscretions. Studies done in the '80s, for example, showed that teenagers were having oral sex back then. These, however, were high school kids, and the practice, Resnick suspects, may have spread more recently to the younger set. Too, Resnick acknowledges that any increase in oral sex could be consistent with the drop in teen abortion and pregnancy; that all of these trends, rather than being contradictory, could be part of the same adaptive behavior.

"In one respect it's probably part of the bigger picture that a growing number of kids in the United States are getting it. They're understanding more about pregnancy prevention and about risk," Resnick says.

But the loose term "oral sex" is itself, I think, imprecise. Among the teenagers I talked to, there was widespread agreement that what oral sex consisted of, in middle school, was girls performing oral sex on boys. "I guess boys think it would be nasty" to perform oral sex on a girl, conjectured one 13-year-old girl. "It's different. It's just—the body parts—it's something different," said one 13-year-old boy, looking a little bit horrified.

Teenagers have been having oral sex for quite some time.

Equally dispiriting, I think, is the striking research, done by a Washington research group called Child Trends, that quantifies the increase in sexual intercourse among girls 13 and 14. "Almost one-fifth of female teens (19 percent) in 1995 reported that they had had sex before age 15, compared with only 11 percent in 1988," noted a recent Child Trends research brief, adding that males did not show a similar increase. ("Sex" is used here to mean intercourse, and does not include oral sex.) For girls at this age, some of the consequences are obvious: increased risk of pregnancy and sexually transmitted disease, because the younger someone starts, the more partners she's likely to have. Sex at this age is also less likely to be consensual and more likely to be coercive; though pressure to have sex often comes from boys in their own age group, it also frequently comes from older boys, and many young girls who do have sex do so with boys who are several years older. According to one study, 24 percent of girls who had sex at age 14 or under reported that it was "nonvoluntary"—basically, rape or molestation.

Other young girls may consent, but only as a result of pressure: "I was just trying to please him," said one 11th-grader I talked to who had had sex for the first time in middle school.

"I regret the age I was when I lost my virginity," said another, who'd had sex with an older guy the summer after eighth grade; when she got to high school, she said, still embarrassed, "everybody knew."

In other words, it would be naive to think that increased sexual activity by young girls is part of some post-feminist equal opportunity movement. I sat in on one sex-ed class where a group of high school girls could not identify the female organ that is "the center of sexual excitement and pleasure" and another where a group of eighth-grade girls all agreed that it was normal for boys to masturbate, but not for girls. In three months of reporting, I heard very few girls make any bold expression of sensuality, apart from one who, during a discussion of risky behavior, timidly expressed the idea that "hugging feels—mmmmmmm!" whereupon she was roundly chastised by her group. One of her classmates pointed out that even hugging can be risky if the boy gets ambitious: "There are some people that be feeling on you when they're hugging!"

Mostly, what I saw was girls being pressured to experiment, in some cases girls curious to experiment, and, invariably, girls condemned when they did. There is still a strong double standard, especially in this age group, that reduces the likelihood that sex, for a girl, is going to feel like an empowered act. Even if she feels empowered doing it, she's unlikely to feel that way afterward, when word gets around.

"If a guy's having sex it's like, oh, who cares," said one eighth-grade girl. "But if a girl is, it's like, oh, she's a slut, she's a 'ho, she's nasty."

"Nasty" and "dirty"

"Nasty" was a word I heard a lot. So was "dirty"—usually used to describe girls who were sexually active or who were suspected of sexual activity, and occasionally used as a way of labeling the boys who pressed girls. "Dirty," of course, has always had a sexual connotation—"dirty old man" being the obvious example—but lately it has acquired a rawer, more literal meaning. Fundamentally, these days, "dirty" means a girl who is suspected of being diseased; likewise, "clean" is a word I heard a lot applied to girls (and, occasionally, boys) who are not having sex and are therefore deemed to be, well, clean.

It made me wonder whether there might be some collateral damage from the war on AIDS and other sexually transmitted diseases; whether heightened awareness of disease—one of the great differences between the sexual climate of the '70s and that of today—might have had some unintended consequences. "We have had a public health/public relations strategy in this country for some time that emphasized not only an erroneously high impression of risk, but that further suggested the universality of risk to all sectors of the population, regardless of their circumstance or specific sexual behaviors," says anthropologist David Murray, pointing out that in this country the risk of heterosexual transmission of AIDS—for example—has sometimes been greatly exaggerated.

"This emphasis has had several very deleterious consequences, not least being the near-hysteria that has sometimes been occasioned in sex education settings."

I wondered whether, as a result, some kids might be overestimating the risk of infection. And whether they were using the information as a way of labeling others, of casting aspersions and besmirching reputations in a way that hurts girls (as matters of sexual reputation usually do) more than boys. I wondered, too, whether our new risk-awareness may be leading boys, particularly older ones, to hit on eighth-graders: Could it be that they think a good way of practicing safe sex is to practice sex on a girl who hasn't had it before?

Extremely disease-conscious

Which is not to say that girls aren't disease-conscious, too. They are. Indeed, it's difficult, I think, to exaggerate the impact that images of disease have had on the mind of any adolescent: To a teenager, the notion of childbearing may seem remote, but the possibility of being, like, gross and smelly and contaminated is easy to comprehend. One day I sat in a sex-ed session where the counselor asked a group of eighth-grade girls to identify the sexually transmitted diseases they knew about; there was hardly one they hadn't heard of.

"Gonorrhea!" they shouted.

"Herpes!"

"AIDS!"

"Shlamidia or something!"

"No, *chlamydia*!"

Though the group was already well-versed, the counselor proceeded to show flip charts of every so-called social disease imaginable: detailed medical drawings of diseased genitalia, rendered with careful attention to ethnic diversity. What was really striking was that, with each new condition, some girl in the group would become convinced that she had it.

When conversation turned to pubic lice, for example, the counselor told them that it's possible to get lice from toilets, and bedding, and even the clothing of other people. Which was all the encouragement the group needed. "There's this girl who used to go to school here," one of the group said, alarmed. "I know now that this girl had crabs. I would let her borrow my clothes and I slept in her bed . . . Is there any way . . . I mean, whenever I got my clothes back I washed them, like, 10 times, but . . . Ooooh! I'm going to the doctor tomorrow!"

Here the girls were taking this information, and their main worry was not only that they'd caught something but they'd caught something from another *female*. Occasionally, girls I talked to expressed fear of catching a disease from a boy, but for the most part girls didn't seem to evaluate boys as possible disease vectors. Sexually active boys were "pretty boys" or "players," but they weren't generally regarded as infectious.

In contrast, when I talked to boys, I found that they, too, worried about disease, but seemed to worry about it mostly in terms of girls who might be disease carriers.

One day I was sitting in the food court at Wheaton [Maryland] Plaza talking to a group of eighth-graders, among them a boy who explained why he chose not to have sex with girls who offered. It wasn't so much a fear of getting a girl pregnant—though that did cross his mind—as fear of an early death brought on by ill-advised contact with a sexually experienced female like, say, any of the more forward 13-year-olds in his class.

"There are so many diseases people are dying of these days," said the boy, shuddering. "HIV, the AIDS disease, herpes." No matter that people are not, in fact, dying of herpes. This boy was convinced that danger lay everywhere around him; that evil sirens beckoned; that, like Odysseus, he'd better lash himself to the mast and sail on by them. Which is why, he said, when certain girls came up to him, or wrote him notes, offering, as some girls do, to perform this or that service, he turned them down. "If they're coming up to you, they must have been used, and they're dirty. I wouldn't do it with them. Not with a nasty, dirty girl."

It would be naive to think that increased sexual activity by young girls is part of some post-feminist equal opportunity movement.

Another day I had a long conversation with one couple, an eighth-grade boy and girl, both children of Salvadoran immigrants, who were notable in their peer group for the fact that they were going steady but not having sex. The girl, whose mother and aunt both have a powerful influence on her, is a determined virgin and the moral compass of the duo; the boy has had sex once, in the sixth grade, with a sixth-grade girl. When I asked him if he used a condom, he said of course; when I asked him who had the condom, he said, to my surprise, that both he and the girl had had one. What had become of the girl he had sex with? He wasn't sure; she'd moved away. Did he come under pressure to have sex with his new girlfriend? Absolutely.

"All my boys get mad at me," he said. "They're, like, 'How can you be going out with this girl for so long? And you don't do anything? When are you going to break up with her?'"

When I asked him why, despite these pressures, he chose a girlfriend who set such strict ground rules, he said that the reason he liked her is because she is, to use his word, "clean."

"It's different with a clean person," he said. "She's still a virgin, and she doesn't do oral sex."

Clearly, the new attention to disease has done a lot of good. Among teens—who *are* at greater risk of getting sexually transmitted diseases, mostly because they are more likely than adults to have multiple partners—the rate of gonorrhea has gone down, though the chlamydia rate has not. But it seems to me that the emphasis on risk has had a couple of not-so-salutary effects: In addition to exacerbating, possibly, the sexual pressure on younger girls—contributing to the stream of come-ons—it has provided yet another way of sorting girls, setting them at odds with one another, dividing them (often with no basis in fact) between good and bad, fast and slow, virgin and whore—and, now, "clean" and "dirty."

In a subtle way, modern scare tactics have lent a new vocabulary—even a fake veneer of legitimacy—to ancient, pernicious stereotypes.

Sexually aggressive girls

"Y'all are going to get *diseases*! Y'all are going to *die*!" a girl who isn't sexually active said one day, talking to two friends who are.

The girls were sitting in a circle of desks, in a classroom of an outer-county middle school. This was another session of the group I'd first encountered during a presentation on contraceptives—the group where two-thirds of the girls admitted to having had sex. In some cases, the girls weren't admitting so much as bragging. And in this—their outspoken sexual aggressiveness—they are part of another relatively new phenomenon that people in the field have begun to notice: a trend of girls who openly pursue sex, brag about sex, lie about sex, boldly offer themselves as sexual objects. It's something that's taking place on all socioeconomic levels, according to Judith Mueller, executive director of the Women's Center in Vienna, Virginia, who says that her counselors see more and more mothers bringing in their daughters for therapy to treat what the mothers perceive, fearfully, as "sexualized behavior."

Which, certainly, is a good term for the swaggering of several girls in this group, which was organized by one teacher, at the request of their school administration, as a way of letting the girls vent about their lives, giving them a chance to talk their way through the fights and arguments and crushes and breakups and slights and tragedies that constitute the daily life of a 13-year-old. This day, they were talking about a party that a classmate was having over the weekend. Two of the girls—I'll call them Girl One and Girl Two—had been plotting sexual strategies over lunch, giggling over acts such as one they called "runnin' a train" (serial sex). They were familiar with the house where the party was going to be held, and during lunch had mapped it like a battlefield: They knew that there was a closet downstairs, which would be available for sexual encounters, and a bathroom ("with a tub!"), and low shrubbery outside. They knew, too, that the mother was going to be upstairs, but reckoned that she wouldn't be coming downstairs much to check.

Mostly, what I saw was girls being pressured to experiment, in some cases girls curious to experiment, and, invariably, girls condemned when they did.

They estimated that there were going to be about 20 girls and 45 boys at the party, including older boys, and that "every boy is going to have to get them a piece." Some of the girls would have to service more than one boy, they figured. There would be lap dancing (where a girl gyrates in a guy's lap) and there would be freak dancing (where a guy stands behind a girl and dances close to her, his crotch against her bottom) and there would be MTV, and BET, and when the teacher asked them whether it made them nervous or not, being shut up in a closet with boys they didn't necessarily know, they found it impossible to take her seriously.

"If you don't want to do something with a guy, he's not going to do it!" Girl One declared.

When the teacher asked them if they'd heard of date rape, she said, "If something happens and a girl screams, people will hear her!"

"How did you get to *be* this way?" another girl asked them, amazed and appalled. Later, she looked at me and asked, sort of desperately, "What do you *think* of us?"

Truly, I didn't know how to answer.

As the girls were plotting their sex games, another girl—I'll call her Girl Three—was sitting quietly. She was one of the girls who had not had sex; earlier, she'd volunteered that she wasn't ready and wasn't interested. Moreover, she said, she was in a steady relationship with a boyfriend who didn't pressure her. She was a small girl, reserved, self-possessed, and something about her self-possession must have deeply irritated Girl One and Girl Two, because they started working on her, urging Girl Three—who couldn't go to the party because she had to baby-sit—to let her boyfriend go to the party without her.

Occasionally, girls I talked to expressed fear of catching a disease from a boy, but for the most part girls didn't seem to evaluate boys as possible disease vectors.

"I think you should allow him to dance and have fun—harmless dancing," one of them said.

Girl Three didn't disagree. He could go to the party. He could dance. "I'm not worried about it," she said.

The next week, I went back, curious to see what had happened at the party. It was hard to get details: Only one group member showed up for that day's session. She had gone to the party, and reported that somebody brought a 24-pack of condoms, somebody else brought a couple bottles of alcohol, but apparently the mom had checked on them more often than they'd expected; at any rate, there had been some freak dancing but then things calmed down, the boys went home and the girls went to sleep.

Something else had happened over the weekend, though. Girl Two had volunteered to perform oral sex on Girl Three's boyfriend; he had accepted and she had done it, had sabotaged Girl Three, the one whose boyfriend didn't pressure her. The teacher, who had already heard about this incident, believed that Girl Three had made the two other girls angry, and that Girl Two had set out to break the couple up.

"I told him," the teacher said, "that he lost a good girlfriend."

Abortion

The sounds can be elemental at the Annandale [Virginia] Women and Family Center, a nurse-run health-care operation that specializes in adolescent health and also, three half-days a week, performs abortions. The day I was there, there was a woman wailing and shouting during her abortion—"Out, out!" it sounded like she was saying—and a nurse was gently saying, to a woman on a gurney, "It's time to wake up!" About a third of the center's abortion clients are teenagers; one, present that day, was a high school senior who described herself as pro-life. She had given speeches against abortion in her high school, she said, but then she had gotten pregnant and there was no steady boyfriend and, well, here she was.

I was there in part because I was interested in the ways states are attempting to regulate abortions performed on minors. In Virginia, as in many states, there is now a law saying that girls under 18 must notify at least one parent before having an abortion. When a girl calls up, the receptionist must now ask how old she is; if she is under 18, the receptionist tells her that she must be accompanied by a parent, or have a signed letter from a parent indicating knowledge of the girl's intent. At some clinics, the receptionist might also point out that the letter doesn't have to be notarized. A girl can interpret this as she wishes. There is no law that says the clinic has to verify the letter she provides.

As it is, however, the law may be more symbolism than substance. Gail Frances, the nurse-practitioner who founded and owns the Annandale center and its Maryland branch, Cygma Health Center, says that most teenagers who come for abortions *do* arrive with a parent and that the youngest often arrive with both, and that this was true before the law took effect. There was the military father, for example, who called up and wanted to know if he could make an appointment for that day; when he brought his daughter in, he insisted that she was only a couple weeks pregnant but the sonogram showed that she was really several months along. This is common: Kids tell their parents they've only missed one period, when in fact they've missed three. Another day, the abortion was for a 12-year-old girl who also had been brought by her father. They had recently immigrated; before their illegal crossing, worried that she might be raped by a border guide, he had shaved her head to make her look like a boy. It hadn't worked, the anguished father said. He was hoping never to have to tell the girl's mother, who hadn't yet joined them in this country.

Talking to kids about sex

I was also there simply to talk to Gail about adolescence, about the kids the clinic sees for ordinary medical appointments, to find out how she advises parents to talk to their kids about sex. Gail, who gives seminars on the topic, is a big advocate of being very explicit with kids; of being precise about terms even at an early age, using words like "vagina" and "uterus" so kids won't grow up thinking precise terms are dirty. As part of the center's outreach, staff members sometimes put kids in one room and parents in another, and inevitably get a "totally different story" from parents and kids about what the kids know and do and wonder about. I'd heard about this technique from other researchers, who say that often when parents are asked whether they talk to their kids about sex, they say "yes." When the kids are asked the same question, they say "no."

Gail and her staff are part of a vast, ideologically conflicted complex of advocates who are trying to help kids in this age group, an agglomeration of teachers, coaches, guidance counselors and church leaders—liberals and conservatives who, for all their strong differences, are alike in their goal of discouraging sex among young teens. Everybody, basically, is for abstinence. The question is how you get there and what you do when that mission fails. They divide themselves, you could say, along a continuum between idealism and pragmatism: idealists being people who believe that young people really can be scared out of having sex and pragmatists being people who believe in dealing with whatever the kids are doing, or might be doing, or someday will do.

"Even if your child is not doing it, if your child is not even thinking about it, you have to realize that your child is still in school with children who are doing it and thinking about it and talking about it," says sexuality counselor Krystal Holland-McKinney. "There are kids who are in the schools French-kissing and touching each other, and your child is exposed to it. You can't hide it."

[Adolescent girls] are part of another relatively new phenomenon that people in the field have begun to notice: a trend of girls who openly pursue sex, brag about sex, lie about sex, boldly offer themselves as sexual objects.

I spent a lot of time with Krystal, who is program director of Florence Crittenton Services in Silver Spring, Maryland. Her organization is an offshoot of the Florence Crittenton homes, which were founded in the 19th century for "fallen and betrayed" (which is to say, pregnant) girls. Reinvented for the new millennium, the Silver Spring branch still offers services to teen mothers, but also conducts 30-week "life skills and comprehensive sexuality education" programs in public schools—sexuality education being a more marketable term than "pregnancy prevention." In the beginning weeks, girls are coached in self-esteem and encouraged to explore their own personalities; the conversations then turn to their relationship with others. Not until spring does the course address sex.

I found Krystal's way with kids to be impressive and instructive. Rather than simply delivering information, she tends to ask a lot of questions: frank, sympathetic, sometimes rapid-fire questions that respect kids' intelligence, avoid judging and encourage them to think situations through. Once, for example, I saw her talking to a 13-year-old girl. The girl, pale and chubby, with long colorless hair that she tended to play with nervously, was in a mall, on a field trip with her sex-ed group. During lunch, she had managed to strike up a conversation with an older guy, a stranger, at a nearby table. Krystal neatly ended that interaction by sliding her lunch tray next to the girl. She almost immediately found out that the girl had what might delicately be called "home issues." The girl, who was white, was going out with an older black guy, and her mother had told her that if she became pregnant by a black man, "she would pull the baby out and stomp it on the ground."

Krystal, who is black, said, "Has your mother had experience with black men that would lead her to think that way?"

"Do you feel badly, the way she talks about black people?"

"Is your dad around?"

"Does he feel the same way?"

"How do you think you will be with your own children?"

As Krystal listened, the girl started talking vaguely about moving out of her house and in with her boyfriend. "If it ends," Krystal asked her, "what will you do then? Where will you go?"

Boys and sex ed

Another time, I watched Krystal working with a group of high school boys who had been brought by their coach. Amazingly, it is rare that anybody pays much attention to boys; there are few sexuality programs for boys, apart from basic health-class sex-ed. This day, Krystal arrived with a game in which she tossed cards with words on them like "vagina" and "testicles" and "fallopian tube" and "semen" on the table and encouraged the boys to pair up the words and explain why they had paired them. She also talked about relationships, asking them if they'd ever had a girl tell them she was pregnant.

"Oh NO!" the boys said, collapsing with laughter.

If a girl said that, Krystal asked them, "what do you think she wants?"

"Some money," said one boy.

"Some support," said another.

She agreed that some girls aren't trustworthy, that some girls sleep around, but if you don't know a girl well enough to know whether she's serious when she says she's pregnant, Krystal wanted to know, "then should you lay down with her?"

She showed them a chart of the female anatomy, saying things like, "Does everyone know what the cervix is?" and then she showed them how the vagina works. To make it really clear she stood up, positioning her own body next to the drawing, and said, "If this is me standing sideways, see how my vagina goes toward the back?" The boys nodded, transfixed: Here was a lady revealing to them the world's greatest mystery. "Do you know how deep a vagina is?"

The boys didn't.

"It's only three or four inches," she said, explaining that sex, therefore, can be very painful for a girl or woman if it goes too fast; or if she doesn't want it; or if she's scared; or if her brain is sending stress messages to her body; but that if a boy proceeds slowly, and gently, the vagina can relax and enlarge.

"So you have to ease up," one of them said.

"That's right," Krystal said.

Identifying who is "at risk"

Afterward, I asked her if there was any way to identify why some young kids have sex and others don't. It's hard, she said. "You can't look at a child and say, 'She's not involved in any of that, she knows where her head is and she knows what her goals are and she's not going to have sex now.'" But she does think certain kinds of kids are more likely candidates for sex: a child who is hanging around with other kids having sex; a child who has a lot of free time and overworked parents and little supervision; or a child "who doesn't have a strong, healthy relationship with at least one parent, where they can talk about what's on their mind and what they're dealing with."

During the time that I'd spent with Krystal and others, it became clear how much the complexity of adult lives affects children. So often, it seemed that a girl who was having sex or was on the verge of giving in to pressure came from a home with a single parent, or a home in some state of emotional chaos. In particular, it struck me that girls who came up to their counselors with really complex, adult-type problems—like one sweet-looking 13-year-old, who approached one counselor to mention that her boyfriend had a baby by a girl who lived in another state, and she'd urged him to stay in contact with the mother of this child but he wasn't really interested, and did the counselor think she should continue going out with him?—were girls who did not live with their own fathers, often girls having problems with stepdads. This was purely an impression. Nothing systematic. But the prophylactic importance of the father is, I think, too often ignored: One study, published last year, indicated that a girl who has a close relationship with her father may actually, *physically,* come into puberty later than a girl who doesn't. Researchers don't know why this happens, but speculate that not having a father around may create stress that pushes a girl into early sexual maturity.

"Parents today discount how important they are to their children and how much their children look to them for values," says Kristin Moore, president of the research group Child Trends, who recommends talking to kids about sex not once but often; talking to boys as well as girls; and being specific. What good, after all, does it do to say to your kid, "Be careful"? Does that mean go to a clinic? Carry a condom? Watch out for predators? Walk on the sidewalk and not in the street?

One girl's story

"I told her that it's very hard getting a job without a high school degree. We went through the whole thing. I said, 'If you ever decide to have sex, I won't be happy with your decision; however, I have to support your decision.' I got her as much information as I could about disease. We talked about condoms, about using it always. That if you ever decide you are ready to have sex, all I ask is that you tell me first. And what did she do? She had sex and didn't tell me!"

This is one mother talking. I'll call her Big D, and I'll call her daughter Little D. The daughter, who is 16, wouldn't mind having her name in the paper, because that's another thing about kids these days—kids will talk with strangers about sex, they'll talk with reporters, and often they are willing to use their names because, hey, the kids on *Real World* have sex and use their names—but the mother, Big D, says no, don't use your name.

They are sitting at a round kitchen table. It is a Saturday morning, early, rainy. The girl is thin, and tall, with wide eyes and hair pulled back in a ponytail; Big D is looking at her fondly. They say they have a great relationship. They talk all the time. Big D is a strict mother, too strict, Little D thinks. She won't let Little D have a pager. She won't let Little D go to a lot of parties. She watches the clothes that Little D wears, and intervenes if she thinks they're too revealing. She gets up early in the morning to go to work, but she always talks to her daughter over breakfast, and she makes sure somebody is there after school. She does everything she can think of. But two years ago, Little D started getting some attention from a guy. An older guy. For three months she resisted. The boy was cute. All the girls were after him. Suddenly, she had a new social cachet! Eventually she had sex with him. She didn't tell her mom. Her friends told her not to tell. "Your friends!" says Big D now.

She didn't like those friends. And it turns out that, because of them, she didn't know what was happening; didn't know that her little girl had sex, and then sat up afterward, and said to the boy, "That's it? That's *all*? I could have waited!"

"What do you mean?" the boy asked.

"It wasn't all that!" she told him.

"You just weren't into it!" he said.

"I was into it!" she said. "It wasn't all that!"

Big D laughs now, despite herself. It was the next boy she caught. One night, she was sitting downstairs and heard some rustling, and she didn't know what it was, but before she went to bed she checked on Little D, as she always does, and there the boy was, in bed with her daughter! He had climbed in through the window! Big D went for the boy, who jumped out the window before he even had a chance to pull his pants up. The next day, she called in reinforcements: Little D's grandmother called her, and her aunt came over, and Big D also made an appointment to have Little D checked by a doctor and tested for AIDS, venereal disease, the whole nine yards. "I'm concerned about pregnancy, but I'm more concerned about AIDS," Big D admits. "You have options with pregnancy. You don't have options with AIDS."

In other words, she has talked, she has done everything. Has it helped? Maybe. Does it matter that Little D doesn't have a father living with her to beat the boys away with a stick? Maybe. The only clear thing is that a girl these days better have a strong inner compass, because the wider culture isn't going to give her one; the pull of peer pressure can be as strong as a riptide. "All I can do is keep talking," Big D figures; today, for example, they are going to talk about Little D's new boyfriend, with whom she is considering having sex. Sitting there looking at her, so beloved by her mother, I think: New boy makes three. How many boys does it take before you go from being thought of as one sort of girl to being thought of as another? As it happens, Little D says, recently a new boy moved in to their school and some ex-friends of hers told him some things about her, and when she called him up he told her what the ex-friends said. That she has a disease. Which isn't true.

"I was, like: 'Think about this!'" Little D says, sitting there at the table, outraged. "'*Think* about what they're saying. Why would they tell you something like that about me? You know they don't like me. Have you ever seen me talking to them?' I'm, like, 'Why would I give that to anybody?' He was, like, 'Where I'm from girls will do that.' I'm, like, 'Girls will do that, I don't care where they're from, but I wouldn't do that.' He was, like, 'Well, I don't know.'"

"I feel bad for her," Big D says. "I told her, people are always going to be saying something. You can't beat yourself up. You have to persevere."

Little D points out, plaintively: "And I only wanted to be friends."

9

Factors That Indicate a Teen Is Not Ready for Sex

Nathalie Bartle with Susan Lieberman

Nathalie Bartle is an adolescent psychologist and associate professor at Allegheny University of the Health Sciences, School of Public Health, in Philadelphia. Susan Lieberman, the author of The Real High School Handbook, *is the director of Leadership Rice, a student-led mentor program at Rice University in Houston.*

Despite their best intentions, some teens may not be willing to wait until they are married to have sex. The decision to have sex is an adult one. Although there is no "right" age at which a person is ready to have sex, there are some characteristics that indicate whether a person has developed the emotional and intellectual maturity necessary to have a healthy and satisfying sexual relationship. If teens are unwilling or unready to discuss the risks, consequences, and responsibilities of sex, they are not ready to have sex.

As one mom acknowledged, despite her best intentions, she worried about the day her daughter "Just got that look in [her] eye" for sex. All of us can surely recollect situations in which we were seduced by desire, but how many of us feel at ease speaking forthrightly about its pull? It is, unquestionably, one of the most perplexing topics for discussion, as these mother-daughter pairs attested. We might say we believe there is something very special about waiting to have intercourse with a husband; we might express the belief that mature women may be ready for sex before they are married but that during high school emotional maturity lags behind physical maturity. Or we may wish to help our daughters define the circumstances necessary for sexual intimacy. Certainly women exhibit great variety in the ways they address desire, and we can only share with our daughters what makes sense for us and why.

Figuring out desire in all its complexity is a slow and perplexing business for many girls. In the process, some girls may jump in simply to be done with the question: "Do I or don't I?" One gift we can give our daughters is an appreciation for the importance of making decisions based on their internal needs and values rather than just on the external situation.

Wishing for a checklist

Katrina wished for a checklist to help her decide when she would be ready for sexual intimacy. The easiest response is "when you are married," but we know this answer will fail to serve a majority of our daughters today. As more and more women postpone marriage until their late twenties, the virtues, both physical and emotional, of abstinence may become more difficult for young women to appreciate. Sexual intimacy, the girls I spoke with understood, brought responsibilities. It demanded emotional and physical readiness, a partner who was caring and respectful, and an inner certainty—all of which resist convenient scheduling.

Many mothers and girls have asked me, "So, when is it okay for girls to become sexually active?" They seem eager to have a specific age delineated, perhaps a specific day that they can mark on a calendar. I wish it were so easy. Of course, there is no "right" or simple answer to this question, because it hinges so much on each individual girl, her past experiences, her current relationship, and a host of other unquantifiable characteristics. As a health care professional, I am aware that many girls do not develop the emotional and intellectual maturity for sex until they are in their late teens or early twenties, and it is my professional opinion that it is best for girls to postpone intercourse until they have reached this level of maturity. Although each girl will make her decisions individually, I do think we can give a young woman some clear cautions about signs that she is *not* yet prepared for sexual activity:

- If she is not ready to go to a doctor and take responsibility for her own contraception
- If she does not feel comfortable discussing sexuality with her proposed partner
- If her proposed partner is not willing to use contraception himself in every sexual encounter
- If she is filled with doubt about what she is doing
- If she feels ashamed about what she is doing
- If she is not willing to be honest with her partner and is not sure of his honesty with her
- If she and her partner have not discussed what they would do if she were to become pregnant
- If she doesn't like her partner's friends and doesn't trust his judgment
- If she has any suspicion that her partner has been sexually involved with others and has not been tested for AIDS
- If she needs alcohol or drugs to make her feel relaxed enough for sex
- If she is responding to someone else's needs and not her own

Even if a young woman feels certain that she is in a loving and caring relationship, knows about contraception and STDs, and has none of the reservations on the above checklist, she still may not possess the emotional sophistication to reach a wise decision about sex. Moreover, a teenage girl can't possibly have the wide-ranging perspective of a slightly older woman, who can compare her current relationship to some others. Too many times I have had a girl tell me how she was certain she had discovered love and instead had gotten pregnant. It can seem to an adolescent, in the rush of emotion, as though a high school sweetheart is the be-all and end-all, the guy she will marry, so why not do it all now? But the majority of women do not marry their high school sweethearts. Rather, they have several different relationships before settling on the one that feels right because it is committed and loving.

> *Many girls do not develop the emotional and*
> *intellectual maturity for sex until they are in their*
> *late teens or early twenties.*

But I also know as a counselor that many girls do choose to become sexually active in adolescence, and they don't appear to be suffering irreparable harm. More than half of our teenage girls have sex by the time they are eighteen.[1] To say that there is no "okay time" for this group defies reality and suggests that a majority of these girls will meet with harmful outcomes. Adolescent girls are having sex and will continue to do so. As a counselor, I try to provide as much information as girls need to determine for *themselves* when the "right time" will be. As Ingrid Shepherd said, "Before I can make a decision I need to know who believes what and why. If I can get someone who believes it's fine to have sex, I'll ask them why. And I'll listen to those reasons and then I'll go to my own parents or someone else who believes you shouldn't, and I'll say, Why? And then I'll think about those reasons—you just have to have a lot of information."

An adult decision

The decision to become sexually active is ultimately an "adult" one. I use this term loosely, just as we do in other areas of society. To drive, you have to be sixteen; to vote, you have to be eighteen; in most states, you have to be twenty-one to drink. We all know that some seventeen-year-olds are more mature than twenty-year-olds, so to try to define an age criterion for sexual activity seems about as helpful as saying, "Just don't do it." But we also know that many adolescent girls are quick to judge themselves as "adults" and are probably naive about the nuances of a fully developed relationship. Mothers can help sort through these considerations by asking whether we consider our girls young adults and whether our daughters agree—about themselves *and* their partners. Such a conversation would seem to me more useful than an age criterion in helping girls determine when it is "okay" to have sex.

Some daughters may express an attraction to other girls. This can be a natural part of adolescence, and a mother can save her daughter enormous pain and self-doubt by opening the door to discussion and listening to her voice. Mothers play a critical role in reaffirming their girl's sense of self, especially as their sexuality unfolds.

We want our girls to know that sexuality will be with them all their lives, that they needn't be impatient to experience sex. The wiser and more confident they become and the more discriminating they are in choosing partners, the more likely it is that their sexual experiences will be positive.

Note

1. U.S. Department of Health and Human Services, *Fertility, Family Planning, and Women's Health*, p. 30. Moore, *Facts at a Glance*; Brown and Eisenberg, *Best Intentions*, p. 96; Carnegie Council, *Great Transitions*, p. 24.

10

Parents Should Talk to Their Children About Sexual Values

Deborah M. Roffman

Deborah M. Roffman, the author of Sex and Sensibility: The Think-ing Parent's Guide to Talking Sense About Sex, *is a consultant on human sexuality education for schools in the Baltimore–Washington, D.C., area.*

Teens are becoming sexually active at young ages and many of their parents are surprised at their children's sexual precociousness. American popular culture surrounds children with sexual images and messages that urge teens to become sexually active. Parents need to become aware of the mixed messages their children are re-ceiving and talk to them about their sexual values. Children need and look for guidance, limits, and values from their parents.

Oral sex and middle schoolers, freak dancing among 10-year-olds, al-legations of rape by boys as young as 9. And recently a lacrosse player at Baltimore's private St. Paul's School secretly videotaped himself having sex with a 15-year-old girl and then played the recording for teammates.

Incidents such as these explode onto the front pages of newspapers like so many grenades, leaving many parents wondering whether the gen-eration gap has suddenly morphed into the Grand Canyon. Baltimore families have watched, incredulous, as the St. Paul's story has unfolded in their morning newspapers, with regular updates on the evening news: The videotape was shown not once but twice, first to a small group, then to a larger gathering of players; according to their coach, none of the boys protested or pushed the eject button; after school administrators learned of the incident, the top-ranked varsity lacrosse team's season was can-celed, some 30 students suspended and the sophomore who made the tape expelled. The whole thing's shocking, isn't it?

Yes. But the shock tells a story in itself. The fact that these examples of precocious, unhealthy sexualization are not on most adults' radar screens—not even in their worst nightmares—speaks legions. For someone like me, who has been teaching about sexuality for more than 30 years, the surprise is in the surprise. What else do we expect in a culture where by the age of 19 our children have spent nearly 19,000 hours in front of the television (compared with only 16,000 hours in school), and where nearly two-thirds of all television programming has sexual content? While I remember school kids 20 years ago consulting Dr. Ruth or the manual *Our Bodies, Ourselves,* even preteens in classes today regularly refer to the likes of Dr. Drew and *Sex and the City* as their expert sources. "Yeah, I heard about that on Jerry Springer," I hear kids say at least once a week.

> *The images and messages our kids see and hear . . . depict sex as recreation, sex as commerce and exploitation, sex as sport, status, and even violence.*

Parents remain pretty much out of the loop. Of course, it's become harder and harder to keep up with a media- and technology-savvy younger generation that is attuned to every nuance of change. But it's also true that we haven't been paying enough attention to what our children are seeing and hearing about sex every day. As Susan Reimer, a Baltimore columnist and mother whom I've come to know well, put it, never in her wildest dreams had it occurred to her that one day she'd have to sit her son down and tell him: "It is wrong to videotape yourself having sex with a minor girl and then entertain your friends with the results!"

She's right, of course. But no matter how attentive adults try to be, we can never anticipate all the situations our kids will face. Instead it's time to take a hard look at the world through our children's eyes, and recognize how these high-profile stories mirror the stark ugliness of a popular culture in which sex has been essentially de-meaned—literally stripped of meaning.

The media's depiction of sex

The images and messages our kids see and hear—on TV and in videos, movies, advertisements and lyrics—depict sex as recreation, sex as commerce and exploitation, sex as sport, status and even violence. Warmth and caring have given way to being "cool" at all costs; mutuality has been replaced by selfish pursuit; the notions of intimacy and commitment have been shelved as cumbersome relics of some bygone era. Just take a look at MTV's *Undressed,* which features scantily clad high schoolers (in lingerie and leather) having sex while their parents are out. It makes my students' open banter about the machinations on *Temptation Island* seem, well, like child's play.

Many students deny that they are affected by sex on television. Recently, one 10th grader in Washington criticized me angrily for even suggesting a link. "How could adults be stupid enough to think that kids are stupid enough to be influenced by what they see on television?" he asked. One girl told me last week, "I only watch *Sex and the City* to see the clothes." But should anyone doubt the power of these crude, dehumanizing messages, consider this: The St. Paul's incident was apparently patterned on a similar event in the film *American Pie,* where a high school student films himself having sex with an unsuspecting girl and broadcasts it over the Internet.

Kids pick up on—and all too often act on—the messages they see and hear around them. Remember the debate about whether oral sex counted as sexual relations that unfolded during the Monica Lewinsky scandal? Many people blamed it for the apparent increase in oral sex among school kids. But truthfully kids have been reacting to far more entrenched and confusing messages. While popular culture glamorizes sex, public service ads warn about the possible dire consequences. The interpretation? As long as you avoid intercourse it's all okay.

"So, what's wrong with an eighth-grade girl having oral sex?" one of my 14-year-old students asked recently, during a discussion about sexual values. It was offered more as a statement than a question. "After all, you can't get pregnant or one of those bad diseases," she went on, as if to prove what she seemed to consider an obvious point. "Besides, it's not really sex. So you're still a virgin. What's the big deal? Teenagers are supposed to experiment. That's just one of the things they might decide to try out."

Children and adolescents are still looking to us, the adults in their lives, for guidance, limits and values.

"Oh, but you *can* get one of those diseases," a classmate retorted, looking startled. Some members of the group nodded. Others looked surprised, but this new piece of information, spoken forcefully by a peer, definitely seemed to register. "Well, I guess that's different then," the first girl said. "I didn't know you could get it that way."

The issue seemed settled, but I was not at all relieved. Should the threat of disease—or pregnancy—be the only limit these students think they have on their sexual experimentation? Not one of them seemed bothered that oral sex had been described as "no big deal," "not really sex" and as a way to hold onto virginity—as if it were a simple rite of passage, like taking a puff of tobacco or a sip of beer.

Mixed messages

It's hardly surprising that students sound so confused when they are learning from a culture that speaks out of both sides of its mouth: Sex is the best thing you can do! Sex is the worst thing you can do! Sex is meaningless! Sex is holy! Sex gets you ultimate approval! Sex gets you ultimate disapproval! Do it now! Save it forever! While the popular culture's message is "Anything Goes," the federal government's is "Abstinence Only."

"Why don't adults make up their minds?" I've heard my students ask more times than I can count.

The mixed messages are everywhere. A clear example caught my eye in a newspaper not long ago. On the very same page as a sober story reporting the increased incidence of oral sex among middle schoolers was a prominent department store clothing ad showing an adolescent, wearing a come-hither pout and baring much of her breasts.

Double standards

Despite the changes I observe in the way kids perceive and talk about sex, one thing hasn't changed at all. There's still a different standard of behavior for boys and girls. Nothing convinces me of this more than the continued use of the double standard's linguistic linchpin—the word "slut."

Listen in on conversations in any school hallway and you'll hear the word bandied about as if the '60s never happened. Its continued use goes a long way toward explaining the astonishing lapses in moral judgment like the one at St. Paul's among boys who were good, decent kids in many other respects. The St. Paul's incident simply projected the same-old, same-old refrain on high-tech footage. Certainly in the aftermath there has been much public condemnation of the behavior of the boys involved, but I've also heard privately—from students and adults alike—another theme: If sex happens, it's the girl's fault. Add to that the sense of celebrity and entitlement that accompanies the so-called jock culture, and the lacrosse players' behavior fits a familiar pattern.

But don't simply blame jock culture—or believe the rest of us can distance ourselves. As David Jackson, head of the Park School in Baltimore (one of the schools where I teach) wrote in a letter of support to his counterpart at St. Paul's: "Many people have approached me with the comment, 'Aren't you glad you are not at St. Paul's?' Although this question is well-meaning, I believe we are all at St. Paul's this week. All of us, teachers and parents, who are involved in raising adolescents today confront these issues."

Lessons learned

When students learn about incidents such as this one, the TV images suddenly take on a frightening tone of reality. There were a handful of kids in my classes (mostly boys) who dismissed the episode as a stupid mistake to which adults foolishly overreacted. But, once nudged beyond gossip, the vast majority have responded with appropriate outrage—as well as heartfelt sympathy for the girl involved. One sixth-grade boy wondered whether she would "be able to trust anyone ever again." A girl acknowledged, "I never thought anything like this could ever happen so close to home."

As I've talked it over with students throughout the Baltimore community, I've realized that, at least in the short run, the incident has helped re-sensitize youngsters to the complexities and vulnerabilities of sex in real life. Many have acknowledged that, yes, it could have happened at their school, too, and that, yes, they, too, might have joined in without thinking. One class of middle schoolers described themselves as changed people because of what they had learned. Others told me that they now understood what the term "sex object" really means.

At the same time, countless parents and teachers have overcome their discomfort, shock and disbelief to use this moment as an opportunity to talk with kids about sex. For many, the tone was set by St. Paul's itself, where administrators not only acted with moral clarity and courage by canceling the lacrosse season, but recognized the need to educate the boys. As the school psychologist Rosemary Hanley said, it is important to help the boys understand how and why "good people can do bad things." In this city, at least for now, the sickness in our society about sex has been thrown into high relief.

But in the long run, it's we parents who can and will make the difference. First we'll have to play catch-up—and do it quickly. According to the Parents Television Council, a nonpartisan group that advocates responsible programming, the number of sexual references on television alone more than tripled between 1988 and 1999, and the pace continues to mount. That means that middle-school children today are growing up in a culture that is different not just from mine, but even from their older siblings'.

Children and adolescents are still looking to us, the adults in their lives, for guidance, limits and values. Believe me. I know these truths directly, from the thousands of young people I've listened to, one-on-one and in classroom discussions. It's up to us to close the gap between what we want them to think about sex and what those who are after their attention and their dollars want them to think. Let's hope it won't take too many more teenage sexual scandals or tragedies before we do.

11

Virginity Pledges Help Delay Teen Sex

Commonweal

Commonweal is a biweekly Catholic magazine.

A study found that teenagers who pledged to remain abstinent until marriage refrained from sexual intercourse for a substantially longer period than teens who did not vow to remain abstinent. Although convincing all teenagers to pledge to remain virgins until marriage is not universally effective, the abstinence movement should be encouraged. Providing information about contraception is not enough to reduce or delay teen sex; teenagers must be given strong moral guidelines about sex.

Strange things do happen. Senator Jesse Helms (R-N.C.), chairman of the Foreign Relations Committee, relented after years of obstructionism and allowed the United States to pay its back dues to the United Nations. If Helms can come to terms with the obvious good the UN represents, perhaps "progressive" educators and other advocates of what is called "comprehensive sex education" will one day come to see the virtue and effectiveness of stressing abstinence in public-school sex education. That day has not yet arrived, however.

"Virginity Pledges by Teenagers Can Be Highly Effective, Federal Study Finds," read the surprising (for some) headline in the *New York Times* (January 4). The new study, conducted by Peter Bearman of Columbia University and Christine Bachrach of Yale, concluded that teenagers who took a pledge to abstain from intercourse until marriage "are much *less* likely" to have intercourse than adolescents who did not pledge. "The delay effect is substantial and almost impossible to erase. Taking a pledge delays intercourse for a long time," the study concludes.

The pledge, an idea originating with the Southern Baptist church, has been taken by nearly 3 million American adolescents. Virginity pledges and other "abstinence-only" programs are particularly controversial when implemented in public schools. Federal funding guidelines, stemming from the 1996 Welfare Reform Act, prohibit such programs from provid-

From "Abstinence, Anyone?" *Commonweal*, January 26, 2001. Copyright © 2001 Commonweal Foundation. Used with permission.

ing students with information about contraception.

The debate over the place of moral norms in sex education has long been contentious. The Left is eager to paint abstinence programs as a scheme by the Religious Right to restore traditional gender roles and sexual morality. Some critics even contend that abstinence-only sex education represents an unconstitutional entanglement of church and state! For religious conservatives, schools that provide information about contraception are seen to be enabling immoral behavior. In addition, comprehensive sex education, with its "nonjudgmental" approach to sexual activity outside of marriage, is rejected as a form of indoctrination in pernicious liberal values.

Teenagers who took a pledge to abstain from intercourse until marriage "are much less likely" to have intercourse than adolescents who did not pledge.

High school students, let alone younger children, should not be engaging in sexual intercourse. The news that abstinence works—even so-called "abstinence-only" programs—should be welcome. The high rates of sexually transmitted disease, HIV, abortion, and unwed motherhood among teenagers in the U.S. has had devastating consequences, especially for young and poor women and their children. However social policy may balance the abstinence message with the provision of contraceptive information, surely abstinence is what most parents and increasingly many professionals think needs to be stressed. Still, the Bearman-Bachrach study has not been greeted with enthusiasm by all. An earlier version of the paper presented at a Planned Parenthood of New York City workshop brought an extraordinary reaction, with the president of SIECUS (Sexuality Information and Education Council of the United States) leading an "Abstinence programs do not work" chant. In other contexts, such a willful rejection of new knowledge is called obscurantism.

Of course, virginity pledges are not the sole answer to teenage irresponsibility in matters sexual. The study also found that pledgers are less likely to use contraception than are nonpledgers when they eventually do have intercourse. Obviously no single approach is appropriate for all kids. Bearman and Bachrach carefully note that the pledge works in specific social contexts. The pledge is more effective with younger teenagers (fifteen- and sixteen-year-olds) and loses its effectiveness altogether if taken by too many or too few adolescents in the same social setting. Once again, attitudes toward sex are shown to be deeply embedded in group norms.

Rates of teenage pregnancy have actually declined since the early 1990s. Despite the continuing political antagonism surrounding this issue, a willingness on the part of liberals and conservatives alike to criticize teenage sex and defend the institution of marriage has helped to stem the tide of destructive behavior among the young. A consensus now seems to exist that "abstinence-plus" or "mixed" programs, curriculums that emphasize abstinence but also provide information about contraception, make the most sense. But the emphasis must be placed unambiguously on abstinence. As historians and social critics like Barbara Dafoe Whitehead have pointed out, the "technological" approach to sex education that predominated in the recent past betrayed a gross misunderstanding of the motivations and dynamics behind teenage sexual activity. Information alone does not improve teenage decision making. Children must have a compelling reason to make use of information, and strong moral guidelines can provide such reasons when it comes to sex. As adults know, sex is as much about the will as it is about the body. Despite the allure of sexual libertinism in the media and larger culture, adolescents still want to understand the meaning of love and marriage. That is where any commonsense approach to sex education should start.

Mocking the efforts of religious conservatives to uphold traditional notions of sexual morality and marriage is too easy. Yes, some of the abstinence-only teaching methods are silly and falsely idealize the complex nature of sexual relations. Marriages, obviously, do not always work out. Premarital sex is not a straight road to perdition. But the so-called enlightened or "recreational" model of modern sexuality is no less idealized and even more misleading. Sex can be a fierce force in our lives, and rarely is it more fierce than in adolescence. Religious tradition and social custom have long recognized the disorienting power of sexual desire in the lives of the young by upholding the ideal of faithful, lifelong marriage, and providing boundaries for courtship. That approach is not just sound morality, but as a growing body of social scientific evidence shows, it is also good social policy.

12

The Effectiveness of Virginity Pledges Is Exaggerated

Susan Dominus

Susan Dominus, a former senior editor at New York Magazine, *is the editor-in-chief of* Nerve *magazine.*

A study that reported on the effectiveness of teen virginity pledges offers mixed reviews about the abstinence movement. While the abstinence pledge was effective at delaying intercourse among sixteen-year-olds, it was less effective among other age groups. The study also found the pledge was less effective if it was taken by too many or too few teenagers at the same time. In addition, abstinence pledges do nothing to lower the teen pregnancy rate, the rate of sexually transmitted diseases, or even rates of sexual experimentation among teens.

It must amaze teenagers that sex education can generate such political firestorms, given how dull it usually is. At my public high school, we took it somewhat less seriously than shop and typing; in shop, at least I learned how to use a C-clamp, but despite the relative candor of our sex-ed curriculum, I can't remember anything useful, much less sexually inspiring, that came out of it. Mostly I remember a film depicting Michelangelo's David, first in his normal state of grace, then suddenly, as the camera zoomed in, very much aroused. I can still hear the cartoony "boing" that marked the transition.

That was a decade or so before the rise of the sexual-abstinence movement, which encourages teenagers to pledge their chastity until marriage and sponsors big conferences at which attendees wear "Stick to your commitment" T-shirts. Its influence has, at least so far, exceeded its membership. Sexy celebrities like Enrique Iglesias and Jessica Simpson have declared their commitment; a 23-year-old Williams graduate named Wendy Shalit published her call for *A Return to Modesty;* and a young Harvard graduate named Tara McCarthy published *Been There, Haven't Done That,* about her decision to remain a virgin despite having been "touched, kissed, poked, prodded, rubbed, caressed, sucked, licked, bitten—you name it." And today, in nearly a quarter of the country's school districts, sex ed comes down to two basic tenets: the only kind of sex that's acceptable is the married kind; the only fact about contraception that's important is that it fails a lot.

The pledge study

Until very recently, however, there wasn't any evidence of what impact all this talk had on teenagers' actual conduct. But in January 2001, two sociologists reported that among teenagers who had never had intercourse, those who made voluntary public abstinence pledges delayed the act about 18 months longer than those who did not make a pledge. Good news for the abstinence movement, right? Actually, the answer—as with all answers that teenagers give about their behavior—is less than straightforward. The pledge was more effective among 16-year-olds than 18-year-olds; there was no entirely conclusive evidence about its effectiveness among 15-year-olds; and it was only effective among those surveyed so long as less than 30 percent of their classmates took it. It had to be popular, but not too popular. Pity the poor policy maker who's supposed to act on these findings, navigating the incomprehensible logic of high-school cliques and identity politics.

It's hard, then, to figure out what the good news is about the abstinence pledge. It's not lower pregnancy rates: one of the study's most disturbing findings was that students who broke the pledge were less likely to use birth control. ("Contraception doesn't concern us," said Jimmy Hester, coordinator of True Love Waits, a pro-abstinence group. "Waiting is what we're striving for here.") For the same reason, it's not lower rates of sexually transmitted diseases. And it may not even be lower rates of experimentation. Did the injunction against intercourse push teenagers to try oral sex (as half of teenage boys have, according to a federally financed study) or anal sex (as 10 percent of boys have, according to the same study)? No one knows. No one asked.

It's hard . . . to figure out what the good news is about the abstinence pledge. It's not lower pregnancy rates.

Abstinence educators are striving for black and white, yes and no. "What part of 'no' don't you understand?" asks one of the movement's slogans. The part of no, some teenagers might answer, that leaves room for substitute sexual behaviors. Is partial penetration covered? Is anal sex? (As for oral sex, the former president of the United States has already delivered his generous verdict.) Teenagers, like everyone else, are masters of sophisticated rationalization about sex—nowhere more so than on the subject of what constitutes virginity. By involving 6,800 students in a survey about sex but asking them solely about vaginal intercourse, the study has reinforced the dangerous notion that other stuff just doesn't count, couldn't really hurt.

No wonder teenagers are drawn to Britney Spears, a proudly self-identifying virgin who practically pole-dances on prime-time TV then says she's waiting for true love. In one navel-baring, camera-ready package, she personifies teenagers' semiotically schismatic world. Like the Sisqo videos they watch, the shampoo commercials they channel-surf past, the Web sites they check out alone in their rooms, Spears saturates kids with sexuality; then, like their teachers, she tells them to guard their chastity.

Depriving kids of practical information

Perhaps it's too much to ask that anyone develop a calm, measured response to the deafening roar of mass culture. But schools seem to want to neutralize its sexual inundation by depriving kids of any practical information about sex. Fighting excess with privation: it's a particularly American foible, like ordering a Diet Coke with your fries, in the hope that one might cancel out the other. In a best-case scenario, the push and pull of these two extremes might lead kids to a reasonable compromise. But in a worst-case scenario, the contradictory messages simply confuse kids, encouraging them to dismiss all cautionary warnings the way coffee drinkers dismiss conflicting reports about the dangers of caffeine.

Still, there's something perfect about the recent news that Madonna, the poster girl for sexual adventurousness who sang coyly about her first time, and Britney Spears, the most celebrated virgin since Joan of Arc who sings coyly that she "did it again," may go on tour together. Both blond, curvy, uninhibited performers, they are not so much twins as mirror images of each other, each reflecting America's unresolved convictions about the role of sexuality in the lives of its ever-more-adult teenagers. If the two singers really want to bring the house down, perhaps they'll end with a rousing duet of Madonna's "Like a Virgin"—whatever that means.

13

Sex Education Encourages Teen Sex

Richard Nadler

Richard Nadler is the editor of KC Jones, *a monthly conservative opinion journal.*

The sexual revolution among teens ended in the 1990s. The number of teens having sex declined, as did the rates of teen pregnancy, birth, and abortion. In addition, teen approval of premarital sex also fell. The credit for these declining numbers goes to programs that teach teens how to resist sexual pressure and to parental disapproval of teen sex. When teens were taught contraceptive use in school-based sex education programs, teen sex increased, as did the rates of teen pregnancy, birth, and abortion.

For sex educators, the '90s were a decade of unrequited love. Academic research discredited their nostrums, and abstinence programs started to receive a respectful hearing. Then came the most crushing blow of all: Sexual activity among teenagers started to decline.

For years, sex-ed advocates had deflected criticism by explaining that teenagers were born to rut. Sure, the number of teenagers having sex was rising every year, in tandem with the expansion of sex education; and yes, these teenagers were having more sex, with more partners, at ever younger ages. But this, they contended, was an inexorable force of nature, and it was wiser to deal with the inevitable consequences than the inscrutable causes. "To do anything less than be explicit about protection is to stand by and let kids literally risk their lives," wrote one sex-ed advocate in 1993. It was an effective argument, recruiting to the cause of sex education and school-based condom distribution not just advocates of youthful sexual freedom but adults who, while perhaps disapproving, accepted parental impotence as a fact of modern life.

Now, however, the sexual revolution is receding among teens. At the start of the 1990s, adolescents were already registering higher rates of disapproval about teen sex than their elder brothers and sisters had. The ratio of teens with multiple partners fell, suggesting casual sex was on the decline. Deeper behavioral changes soon followed. Major social-science surveys recorded significant reductions in the percentage of sexually experienced teens. One study showed an 11 percent decline between 1991 and 1997. By 1996, teen rates of pregnancy, birth, and abortion had receded from their previous highs by 17 percent, 18 percent, and 37 percent, respectively. The biggest improvements took place among younger teens. From 1988 to 1998, the National Survey of Adolescent Males recorded a 17 percent decrease in sexual experience among 15- to 17-year-old boys.

Confronted by what it once deemed impossible, the sex-ed establishment is taking a new tack. All this good news, they explain, proves they were right all along. Donna Shalala, the secretary of Health and Human Services, attributes the fall in teenage births to both increased abstinence and the "dramatic increase in contraceptive use at first intercourse." This is a bit like crediting both cigarettes and hoses for putting out a fire. Let's try to tease out cause and effect with more precision.

Sex education programs

During the '70s and '80s, sex education became near-universal in the public schools. Most programs were based on a model developed by the Sexuality Information and Education Council of the United States (SIECUS). Under this model, school-based sex education had to be comprehensive so that kids could reach sensible decisions on sexual conduct. "Limiting the adolescent's tendency to explore, question, and ultimately come to his or her own conclusions stifles autonomy and a sense of self," wrote sex educators Susan Wilson and Catherine Sanderson. Shorn of ignorance and fear, kids can learn to enjoy sex without guilt or danger. A SIECUS expert recommended "teaching teens about oral sex and mutual masturbation in order to help them delay the onset of sexual intercourse."

Yet, according to this school of thought, detailed information is not so crucial for parents. "While it is generally desirable for parents to be involved in their children's contraceptive decisions," states a SIECUS position paper, "the right of each person to confidentiality and privacy . . . is paramount."

The results of this approach are now obvious, seen in the number of unplanned pregnancies, aborted fetuses, and welfare dependents. One SIECUS prediction, however, did prove correct: Sex ed increased the rate of contraceptive use among teens. But as teen "autonomy" trumped teen precaution, rates of sexual precocity rose even faster. While sex educators and the media obsessed over increased access to contraception, unwed teenaged girls were conceiving at record rates. Worse, the most rapid growth in sexual activity took place among the youngest teens. These teens use contraception erratically. The Centers for Disease Control reported that girls aged 15 to 17 were more than twice as likely to "miss" two or more birth-control pills per cycle as 18- and 19-year-olds.

So, can increased teen sexual activity fairly be attributed to sex ed? Yes, it can. Researchers have found that instruction in sexual biology and birth control is associated with earlier ages of first intercourse. When adults teach kids how to have sex, how to use contraceptives, and where to get them, the kids simply have more sex. And this approach is the heart and soul of sex-ed ideology.

For Carol Everett, who ran a chain of abortion clinics in the Dallas area, school-based programs were an investment. "When I went to those schools," she says, "my agenda was very clear. The first thing was to get the students to laugh at their parents, because if they laughed at their parents with me, they would not go home and tell their parents what I told them. . . . I'd say, 'Would your parents help you get on a method of contraception if you decided to become sexually active? Don't worry about that, here's a card, come to me.' And the next day . . . the telephone would start to ring." Everett, now a pro-lifer, says, "I knew that anytime I went to a school, the pregnancy rate went up sharply. I knew that by my own statistics. I knew that by working with Planned Parenthood, and by reading their statistics." More pregnancies meant more abortions.

A 1993 study by Leighton Ku and others suggested that the most effective method in reducing teen sex activity is not comprehensive sex ed but the teaching of resistance (say-no-to-sex) skills. Another major study found that delayed sexual debuts are associated—surprise, surprise—with "high levels of parent-family connectedness [and] parental disapproval of their adolescent being sexually active." In perhaps the unkindest cut of all for the sex-ed establishment, the study noted that parents' "disapproval of their adolescent's using contraception" is "the strongest family variable counter indicative of teen pregnancy." Indeed, this disapproval is more protective against pregnancy than "effective contraceptive use [at] first/last sex." Other factors that have been found to delay intercourse include religious faith, an intact, two-parent household, a mother at home, and a "pledge of virginity."

This emerging portrait of effective sex education looks less like the SIECUS guidelines than like a Christian Coalition broadside: authoritative adults, buttressed by faith and moral absolutes, instilling in children pride in sexual purity and disapproval of promiscuity. Still another study found that the proportion of high-school girls learning resistance skills increased from 62 percent to 90 percent between the late '80s and 1995.

When adults teach kids how to have sex, how to use contraceptives, and where to get them, the kids simply have more sex.

The final reason to doubt Shalala's contention that the decline in teen pregnancy can be attributed to a "dramatic increase in contraceptive use" is that, in fact, teen contraception did not become more effective in the '90s. Yes, condom use went up, but this was more than offset by the declining use of the birth-control pill. From 1988 to 1995, the percentage of currently sexually active 15- to 19-year-old females using the pill decreased from 59 to 45, while the percentage using male condoms increased from 33 to 37.

According to Contraceptive Technology, the authoritative source on contraceptive-failure rates, the typical user of birth-control pills has a 5 percent chance of getting pregnant over the course of a year; her chances rise to 14 percent if instead she relies on condoms. And condom awareness has done nothing to reduce the riskiest behaviors. The percentage of sexually active 15- to 19-year-olds using no contraception was 19 percent in 1988 and 19 percent in 1995.

In short, the big change among teens in the '90s was not better contraception, but better morals. Fewer adolescents had intercourse, particularly those 17 years and younger. And those who did have intercourse had it less frequently, and with fewer partners. Less sex meant fewer pregnancies, births, and abortions.

Go figure.

14

Teens Need More
Sex Education

Lisa Collier Cool

Lisa Collier Cool is a widely published author of books and articles whose work has appeared in Cosmopolitan, Glamour, Harper's, Playgirl, Working Mother, *and other periodicals.*

Boys and girls who are barely past puberty are part of a horrifying trend of young children who are becoming sexually active. Parents who are concerned about teen sex are asking schools to offer sex education classes to their children starting in younger grades. Frequently, children are already sexually active by the time their parents and schools begin to discuss sexuality with them. Many children are getting their information about sex from television, the Internet, and their friends. Children and teens who receive accurate information about sex and values from their parents and schools are more likely to abstain from sexual activity than those who do not receive such information.

Thirteen-year-old Ashley Robinson* began dating in fourth grade. At first, "it was movies, malls and making out," says the eighth-grader from Pleasantville, New York. These days, "about half of the people in my class are sexually experienced. Some have lost their virginity, but most have oral sex. It's popular because you can't get pregnant." Last July, she decided to try oral sex with a boy she'd been seeing for a month. "We did it to each other; it was fun. Now we do it at his house, my house, everywhere. Oral sex rules!"

A horrifying trend

Robinson and her friends are part of a horrifying trend. Increasingly, children barely past puberty are sexually active, says Sarah Brown, director of the National Campaign to Prevent Teen Pregnancy (NCPTP), in Washington, D.C. By the time kids turn fifteen, according to research from the

*Names have been changed to protect privacy.

National Center for Health Statistics, one third of girls have had sex (compared with less than 5 percent in 1970), as have 45 percent of boys (up from 20 percent in 1972).

But even those kids who remain virgins aren't necessarily innocent. In a survey by *Seventeen* magazine, 55 percent of teens, aged thirteen to nineteen, admitted to engaging in oral sex. Half of them felt it wasn't as big a deal as intercourse—a view Sarah Brown often hears from kids. "It didn't help that we had a president who said oral sex isn't sex," she says. Adds Robin Goodman, Web site director of New York University's Child Study Center, in New York City, "Oral sex is like the latest sport, an activity kids egg each other on to try. Parents may say, 'That's not my child,' but nearly half of them are wrong."

> *More than three-quarters of parents of kids in seventh to twelfth grades said they wanted schools to offer more detailed information in sex-education classes.*

Recent scandals highlight the extent of the problem. In 1998, parents of as many as fifteen eighth-graders at Williamsburg Middle School, in Arlington, Virginia, were aghast when school officials informed them that their kids were having oral sex at parties and in local parks. (Apparently, a child had confided in a school counselor.) Also that year, a twelve-year-old girl and thirteen-year-old boy were arrested for allegedly organizing an oral-sex-for-hire ring at Langston Hughes Middle School, in upper-middle-class Reston, Virginia. The boy was convicted and sent to a juvenile-detention center, and the girl was placed under house arrest. And in suburban Rockland County, Georgia, more than two hundred children—some as young as twelve—were exposed to syphilis through group sex in 1996. Local health officials were appalled by reports of fourteen-year-olds with as many as fifty sex partners, and girls who engaged in sexual activities with three boys at once.

Deborah Roffman, author of *Sex and Sensibility: The Thinking Parent's Guide to Talking Sense About Sex* (Perseus Publishing, 2001) and a sex educator, has heard similar stories. "There have always been some middle-school students who talk about oral sex, but now there's a surge in kids who actually do it," she says.

Meanwhile, schools are hearing from parents who worry that their kids aren't being taught enough about sexuality. In a recent Kaiser Family Foundation (KFF) survey, more than three-quarters of parents of kids in seventh to twelfth grades said they wanted schools to offer more detailed information in sex-education classes. They want their kids to learn how to obtain and use birth control and deal with the pressure to have intercourse.

The price of preteen intimacy

Not surprisingly, children often regret having sex too soon. In a recent NCPTP survey, 73 percent of twelve- to fourteen-year-olds who had lost their virginity said they wished they'd waited. That sentiment is shared by 58 percent of sexually experienced fifteen- to seventeen-year-olds.

When *Ladies' Home Journal* conducted a survey of kids on the NCPTP Web site, many described their first sexual experience the way fifteen-year-old Jennifer Jacobson* does: "It was the stupidest mistake I ever made." At age twelve, "I snuck out of my house to have sex with a fifteen-year-old guy I'd known for only about a week," she says. "Now I'm going to have to spend the rest of my life trying to forgive myself."

Judy Kuriansky, Ph.D., host of a call-in radio show for teens and author of *Generation Sex: America's Hottest Sex Therapist Answers the Hottest Questions About Sex* (HarperCollins, 1995), sees even more serious repercussions. "Often, a lack of self-esteem makes kids experiment with sex," she says. "Frequently, the result is guilt and shame. As adults, they may punish themselves for their past by not letting themselves enjoy sex. Or they may have trouble establishing meaningful relationships because they've disconnected sex and love."

Girls are especially at risk. Tara Thrutchley, eighteen, a volunteer peer educator for AID Gwinnett, a nonprofit HIV awareness group in Lawrenceville, Georgia, has noticed that girls tend to give oral sex more than they receive it. "A lot of eighth-grade girls engage in this activity with high-school boys," she says. "They see it as a way to please a guy without losing their virginity."

The consequences can be dire. "Girls may become vulnerable to exploitative relationships, especially when they're involved with older boys," says Michael Resnick, Ph.D., professor of pediatrics and director of the National Teen Pregnancy Prevention Research Center, at the University of Minnesota in Minneapolis. "They expect emotional intimacy but don't necessarily get it. That can lead to emotional distress, as well as substance abuse."

Surrounded by sex

What's behind this alarming trend? Virginia Navarro, Ph.D., assistant professor of educational psychology at the University of Missouri, in Columbia, says our sex-saturated culture pushes kids to grow up too fast. "Children's stores and catalogs sell junior versions of sexy styles," she explains. "You see silky bras and panties for five-year-olds and skintight Lycra tops and slit skirts that make prepubescent girls look provocative."

Adding fuel to the fire are racy TV shows like *Dawson's Creek* and *Popular*, which depict teen sex as exciting and normal. More than half of all TV shows include sexual content, with the average prime-time program featuring five or more sexual references per hour, according to a recent study by KFF. Only 9 percent of these widely watched shows ever mention responsible behavior, such as abstinence or using contraception.

The Internet is also swarming with sex. In a recent survey of fifteen hundred kids by the National Center for Missing and Exploited Children, in Alexandria, Virginia, one quarter reported having accidentally stumbled upon pornography while Web surfing or opening e-mails.

But the media is only half the problem, says Resnick. "The majority of parents are squeamish about discussing contraception and doubly squeamish about oral sex," he says. "So, at puberty, young people with natural curiosity about sex encounter uncomfortable silence from their parents instead of guidance."

Megan Ruggiero,* thirteen, an eighth-grader from Armonk, New York, and Kim Abrams,* sixteen, of New York City, say sex and its risks were never discussed in their homes. In Ruggiero's case, suggestive material on the Internet and sex scenes on *Dawson's Creek* "made me think about doing it." Curious, she performed oral sex on her date at a New Year's Eve party last year, an act she says she regrets.

Abrams engaged in oral sex—an activity she now calls disgusting—two years ago, then intercourse, which was also unpleasant. "I started doing things I shouldn't have been doing," she says.

Beth Risacher, a program coordinator at a state agency, in Indianapolis, understands parents' reluctance to discuss sex with their children. "Kids at this age are so sensitive that if you don't take the right approach, they don't listen or they think you're accusing them of something," she says. She waited until her daughter, Elizabeth, was fourteen before discussing AIDS, contraception and sex. Soon afterward, Elizabeth asked for birth control pills, says Risacher. "That's when I found out she'd been having sex since she was only thirteen."

Schools should introduce sex ed at the beginning of middle school and expand the range of topics covered.

Fifteen-year-old Adam Dennison,* of Brooklyn, New York, says his parents would be shocked if they knew that he started having oral sex two years ago. About 75 percent of his friends also do it, he estimates, adding, "I learned most of what I know from my older brother and *Sex and the City*."

While some parents buy into the myth that talking about sex encourages experimentation, the opposite is true, says Debra Haffner, author of *From Diapers to Dating: A Parent's Guide to Raising Sexually Healthy Children* (Newmarket Press, 2000) and past president of the Sexuality Information and Education Council of the U.S., in New York City. "The research is clear: Giving preteens accurate information and sharing your values makes them more likely to abstain."

Leaving children in the dark can promote risky behavior, says Resnick. "Most kids think oral sex is safe because they aren't told that it can lead to sexually transmitted diseases [STDs]," such as gonorrhea, syphilis, chlamydia, HIV, human papilloma virus and possibly hepatitis C, he explains. Nearly all of the kids with whom *Ladies' Home Journal* spoke believed the practice posed little danger. Meanwhile, four million teens contract an STD each year; some from oral sex.

Sex ed: Too little, too late?

Although the U.S. has among the highest rates of STDs and teen pregnancy of any modern country, 7 percent of schools offer no sex education at all and 35 percent limit teachers from discussing contraception and safe sex. "Abstinence until marriage" courses have become common since the government launched a $250 million program in 1996 to pay for them. A Centers for Disease Control and Prevention study shows that only 17 percent of teachers inform junior-high students about the proper use of condoms and just 37 percent do so in senior high.

This trend alarms Susan N. Wilson, executive coordinator of Network for Family Life Education at Rutgers University's School of Social Work, in Piscataway, New Jersey. "It's dangerous in a world where STDs kill young people," she says. A recent study by the Alan Guttmacher Institute, in New York City, shows that nearly three out of ten teachers nationwide work in schools that don't offer sex-ed classes to fifth- and sixth-grade students. Among schools that do, subjects tend to be limited to puberty, the transmission of HIV and abstinence.

Wilson believes that schools should introduce sex ed at the beginning of middle school and expand the range of topics covered. "Our silence is creating dangerous myths," she says. "There should be a wake-up call—withholding crucial information about sexual risk doesn't make our kids safer. Telling them the truth does."

15

Gay Teens Face Unique Challenges

Paula Schleis and Kim Hone-McMahan

Paula Schleis and Kim Hone-McMahan are reporters for the Akron Beacon Journal *in Ohio.*

Gay teenagers face many difficulties about their sexuality. Their family, friends, teachers, and church are often unable to accept their homosexuality. Because of their fears about being condemned because of their sexuality, gay teens sometimes remain in the closet and are therefore unable to meet other gays who could help them come out, meet others like them, and provide role models. Because homosexuality is often either persecuted or ignored by society and schools, many gay teens become deeply depressed and some even attempt suicide. In addition, gay teens often lament missing out on the relationships and experiences their heterosexual friends enjoy. However, despite living in the shadow of fear and shame, many gay teens are hopeful of finding acceptance and tolerance in their future.

S cott's chances for having a normal, happy childhood ended the day he discovered a secret about himself.

It's a secret the 17-year-old still works diligently to bury, yet it's one that occupies his every waking moment.

You see, Scott is gay.

He didn't ask to be gay, he will tell you, and he doesn't know why he is. Who would he ask?

He's never heard a teacher explain it, and if he sought the answer in the 13-year-old health books used at Garfield High School [in Akron, Ohio], it would tell him he's just confused about gender roles.

His classmates? They use the term "faggot" repeatedly, tell gay jokes and taunt anyone considered "different."

His family? No way. It's clear they think homosexuality is disgusting, and a brother he loves reacts with pure hatred when the subject comes up in conversation.

His church? It's only a reminder that people think he's going to hell.

There are many people who would tell Scott being gay is as natural as being born left-handed. That many major religions no longer think it's a sin. That stories of gay couples living happy, productive lives are legion. But Scott's closeted life has not enabled him to meet such people.

Ashamed, fearful, and confused

Ashamed, fearful and confused, Scott prays each night that when morning comes, he won't be gay. But he wakes after another tormented night, and nothing has changed.

The real shame is that Scott is not alone. Far from it.

Most surveys on the topic indicate that about 10 percent of the American population is gay. Others have challenged that statistic, saying their polls put the count at closer to 2 percent.

Many are living the same tortured existence that Scott is because as minors, they are totally dependent on the adults around them. And they see few, if any, allies among them.

Thirteen gay youths were interviewed about what it has been like growing up. Though found through a variety of sources, and representing different backgrounds and circumstances, their stories are strikingly similar.

Perhaps most alarming of all is that nine of them tried to find peace at the edge of a razor, with a handful of pills or at the end of a rope. The other four said that while they never attempted to take their lives, thoughts of suicide were never far away.

While adult gays have the freedom to seek support in adjusting to their sexual orientation, gay children are almost totally ignored—at the very time that their sexuality is developing.

A life and death issue

"Homophobic positions kill people, literally," said Rabbi David Horowitz of Akron, who, along with his wife, Toby, became gay activists after learning their daughter was a lesbian.

"This is not a theoretical debate. This is an issue of life and death," he said.

One expert who participated in a U.S. Department of Health and Human Services task force in 1989 concluded that nearly a third of teen suicides are committed by gay youths. Some groups have challenged that statistic as not being scientific, but no one else has attempted to conduct a similar study.

Local interviews support the idea that gay teens are living very fragile lives. Most of the teens' names in this series have been changed to protect their identity. A few even asked that their schools not be identified.

Eric, Dan, Adam, Angela, Marie and Johnnie—ages 16 through 18—all tried to take their own lives. David, 26, tried to kill himself as a teen, as did Antonio, now 23, who was hospitalized twice while in high school for attempting suicide.

Leonard Jenkins tried to hang himself when he was just 14. Robbie Kirkland killed himself last year at age 14.

Karen Cimini, a psychologist with the Akron Family Institute, said slaying the ghosts that haunt these children is not easy.

"The depression (that they experience) is not something wrong with the brain. It's living oppressed," Cimini said. "Most of the gay people that I see are not significantly ill—they are suffering from the culture they live in."

Most of the students said their parents still don't know the source of their depression. They fear that by revealing they are gay, they risk losing the very love that is now so evident in their parents' concern for them.

While Timothy didn't act on thoughts he had of killing himself, he did do something else that is common among gay teens. He abused his body, cutting his chest, thigh and calf.

"It was a drug because, you see, physical pain stunts all of the emotional pain," explained the 17-year-old Canton Timken High School student.

Adam, a 17-year-old student in a suburban Stark County school, revealed several discolored marks on his skin and explained how he used to burn himself with matches.

Gay teens dread persecution in every aspect of their lives—including family and religious institutions— but many say they feel it most acutely at school.

Eric, 17, of Akron, used to cut himself just deep enough to draw blood. It took his mind off of what was going on in his head, he said.

Gay teens dread persecution in every aspect of their lives—including family and religious institutions—but many say they feel it most acutely at school.

The teen years are a difficult time for many students. It's a time when peers become more influential than family. It's a time when children are questioning who they are and what they want to be.

And they're in a school environment that is less than kind to those deemed to be different. Something as simple as acne or a lisp will draw taunts from classmates.

Most children can take their pain home and be reassured by their parents that they are beautiful just the way they are. Historically when there's persistent abuse, parents—from African-Americans to those who have children with disabilities—have bonded together to force schools to improve the environment for their children.

Gay students, however, keep the pain to themselves. Even if their families knew what they suffered, the teens said, they feel certain their parents would be too ashamed of them to do anything about it.

Hiding their homosexuality

So most gay teens devote their energy to hiding their sexual orientation.

They may pretend to have a steady of the opposite sex, someone who attends another school.

"When friends at school talk about what they did over the weekend,

I'll say something like, 'Me and my boyfriend went to the movies,'" said Jennifer, a junior at an Akron high school.

Many will date the opposite sex, but say maintaining steady relationships when there is no sexual attraction causes an anxiety of its own.

Matthew, 20, a graduate of Stow High School, said he suffered migraine headaches for a year as he tried to keep a steady girl. After they broke up, his migraines went away.

Most gay teens devote their energy to hiding their sexual orientation.

"I'm convinced not being true to myself had caused me physical pain," he said.

The teens lament that they can't enjoy the normal growing-up experiences their heterosexual counterparts enjoy.

At 17, Adam has never had his first date, his first kiss.

"Seeing all of the kids at school holding hands—and having a relationship—that's really hard on me," said Adam, who described himself as a hopeless romantic. "I haven't got to experience the things you're supposed to experience as a teen."

They can't talk about their love interests, and most would never dare attend a prom or other school event with a date.

They work so hard to conceal their orientation, they can't even turn to each other for support.

There are several gay students at Garfield High School, yet when asked how many he knew, Scott said he suspected only one other.

Gay teens may appear as homophobic as any other student, laughing at gay jokes in the cafeteria or snickering when students direct the word "fag" at someone else.

And it's not always a show. Because many of the gay adults who could serve as role models are deep in their own closets, the first gay people many teens are exposed to are media stereotypes: drag queens in the movies, pedophiles in the news or flamboyant couples on talk shows.

The teens often became fearful of what they thought they had to become.

"I hated gay people," said Antonio, a graduate of Cuyahoga Falls High School. "In junior high, I even would make fun of someone who was gay to take attention away from myself."

School

Despite their efforts to melt into the crowd, many gay teens say classmates end up suspecting them anyway.

Eric said he suffers taunts all the time.

"They call me names and say stuff, but I just ignore them," he said.

Adam said that last year, students targeted him constantly. "They just knew that I was 'the fag,'" he said. And they reminded him five to 10 times a day, usually in the hallways between classes, and always loud enough so that everyone would hear.

Sometimes, the students said, the abuse gets physical—a shove in the hallway or a sucker punch on the way home from school—and almost always out of view of adults.

But the slurs aren't always out of adult earshot, and gay teens are acutely aware of how school staff deal with such incidents.

Teachers and administrators usually stop the use of the term "faggot" if they hear it, the students said. Officials rarely admonish a student for using the term, "That's so gay,"—meant to describe anything strange, bad or disgusting, the teens said.

Schools throughout the region reported they deal with gay slurs as they would any kind of verbal harassment. Offenders face anything from mediation to suspension, officials say.

The teachers "don't really ignore it, and they will give warnings, but that's all. They never follow through," said Scott.

What they perceive as a lack of seriousness by the adults in their schools has stopped many gay teens from confiding in counselors.

"I don't trust anyone," said Jennifer, a 16-year-old junior attending an Akron high school.

When the going gets really tough, many teens simply stay home.

Cynthia Loukas, an art teacher at Canton Timken High School, has noticed many of the young men who she suspects are gay are repeatedly truant. "They tend to avoid the situation," she said.

And when it gets intolerable, some just drop out of school.

Johnnie, a student at Garfield High School, said classmates tormented him emotionally and physically for years. In his freshman year, he said a staff member told him that people in gym class were complaining "about a gay person changing in the same room with them."

Because most schools don't teach about what it is to be gay, their silence often fuels the confusion gay teens have about themselves.

Johnnie didn't make it through his freshman year. He dropped out of school for two years.

He has returned to Garfield and, to his surprise, has found a much-improved environment. But each day is still touch and go.

He said he'll count his blessings if he can just get through school without getting beat up. "I don't care if people don't talk to me, but don't come after me," he said.

Most of the gay teens reported being able to find a teacher they could confide in. But school officials said they were not aware of any problems facing gay students.

And in terms of curriculum, support groups or other forms of gay awareness, a survey of districts in the five-county area revealed no district tackling the issue in any significant way.

"Has this district done anything to address an issue of this nature? No," said William Stetler, superintendent of the Lake school district in Stark County. "Has it ever come up in a meeting or discussion? No."

Akron Superintendent Brian Williams said he has never had a counselor or principal or any other staff member suggest changes in curriculum or in-service teacher training or awareness programs for students.

"I have a job that is loaded with duties . . . and you tend to put your priorities where the issues have surfaced," he said.

Garfield High School counselor Vicky Jarvie said she has had students talk with her about their sexuality, but more in terms with their home life. "They've never said they were having any big problem with the school population."

Because most schools don't teach about what it is to be gay, their silence often fuels the confusion gay teens have about themselves.

Jennifer, 16, said she started realizing she could be attracted to females two years ago when she found herself falling in love with a girlfriend. She was confused and ashamed. She knew of a lesbian relative, so she figured it must be hereditary.

Matthew said he knew he was attracted to other boys in the fourth grade. It wasn't until high school that he realized most boys didn't feel the way he did.

"I would stay up crying at night, wondering what was wrong with me," he said. That's when high school became almost unbearable. "I couldn't wait to get out."

A growing awareness

Change is slow, but Wooster High School Principal David Burnison said that every once in awhile, something happens to remind him there are gay teens in his school.

He recalled two girls who attended the prom and took a little ribbing from a staff member who thought they were just joking. When the girls took offense, he had a talk with the staff member.

"We can't assume this is a joke," he said. The issue brought home to him the fact that "maybe we aren't as aware in the schools as we ought to be of the issues of gay students."

Burnison said he got another awareness nudge this year when he caught two girls kissing in the hallway. He said he didn't know they were both girls when he stopped them to prod them along to class, but was satisfied he handled them the way he would have handled any kids trying to sneak a kiss between classes.

In general, experts and gay adults say they advise children to save their coming out process for adulthood and to use their teen years to learn about themselves and how to be comfortable with their sexuality.

Cimini, the psychologist, said she does more than advise.

"I tell them, beg them, plead with them, not to come out in high school, because it's dangerous," she said. "Gay bashing is primarily done by males, 16 to 19."

Coming out

Even when it's not dangerous, gay teens risk losing close friends if they come out of the closet.

Antonio, the Cuyahoga Falls graduate, said he devised a little game with a close Christian friend. How would she feel if he got drunk and killed someone with a car? Could she forgive him if he had raped a girl? What would she think if he were gay?

"Being gay was worse than anything else I could dream up," he said. "It was the one thing she said she couldn't forgive. I was crushed."

Dan, 18, said when a fellow Northwest High School student forced him out last year, he tried denying it for awhile, then gave up.

"I figured I could be a gay guy and a liar, or just a gay guy," he reasoned.

His honesty cost him the friendships of all of the students in his morning prayer group. But in hindsight, that wasn't such a bad thing, he said.

Now that he's out of high school, Dan said he's been able to surround himself with people who truly care about him. He no longer takes depression medication, his suicide attempt last year is a distant memory, and he's involved in a loving relationship where both families have learned to accept him and his partner.

"I feel so much stronger now," he said.

Other teens report that when they have confided in an adult or a friend, it's had a healing effect.

Scott, the Akron Garfield student, said he felt a burden lifted when he came out to a few close friends and found acceptance.

And he noticed his personality changed. "I was always sarcastic before. I never did anything nice to anybody. I figured I was just giving them back what they gave me," he said.

Most of the students at Timothy's Stark County school know he is gay. Despite a couple of fights soon after he came out and a teacher who told him he was going to hell, he feels safe at school and finds the level of support he gets "amazing."

As a result, he said his emotional problems are "getting better by leaps and bounds."

"I'm perfectly proud of being gay," he said.

Timothy also believes that his coming out has paved the way for other gay students at his school who want the freedom to be themselves.

Despite the shadow they live under, many gay teens see glimpses of hope, like comedian Ellen DeGeneres coming out on her television sitcom, and the success of gay musicians like Elton John and Melissa Etheridge.

But they are equally realistic.

"Acceptance takes a long, long time," said Timothy. "I probably will never see total acceptance in my lifetime, so I'll just push for tolerance."

Antonio, 23, and Matthew, 20, represent the light at the end of their dark tunnel.

Both said their teen-age years were full of heartaches and tearful nights. Both hid their secret from close friends and family members until they were out of high school.

But as students at the University of Akron, they found support through the gay student union, they found each other, and they found the courage to come out of the closet.

Now, most members of their families accept them. Through the university group, they are helping several area teens survive their high school years.

"It seems so bad in high school, but it's gonna get better," Antonio tells those students who think they can't make it.

16

Distributing Condoms in Schools Encourages Teen Sex

John D. Hartigan

John D. Hartigan is a corporate lawyer who works in the fields of public health and education.

Studies show that distributing condoms to teenagers in schools does not protect them against sexually transmitted diseases or pregnancy. Teens do not have the discipline or control to use condoms correctly every time they have sex. Other studies have found that teens who have access to condoms in schools increase the level of their sexual activity, thereby increasing their risks for contracting STDs or becoming pregnant.

The theory generally advanced to justify distributing condoms to teenagers is that this will protect them against pregnancy and HIV infection if they choose to be sexually active. However, study after study shows that this policy just doesn't work in practice. In real life, handing out condoms to teenagers is a prescription for disaster.

The main reason for this is that teenagers are simply too impulsive and undisciplined to use condoms with the rigorous care needed to avoid failure. A 1988 survey conducted in the United States revealed that more than 27 percent of all never-married, low-income teenage girls who depend on condoms for birth control become pregnant in their first year of condom use.[1]

To make matters worse, supplying teenagers with condoms inevitably produces a marked increase in their sexual activity. For example, when San Francisco's Balboa High School started giving students coupons that they could exchange for condoms at a nearby city dispensary, the percentage of female students engaging in sexual intercourse jumped by one-fourth in just two years.[2] Similarly, a study of adolescents taking part in a three-year condom promotion experiment in Switzerland showed that the proportion of girls under the age of 17 engaging in sexual activity increased by almost two-thirds—from 36 to 57 percent.[3]

Given these inherent drawbacks, it is hardly surprising that school-

"The Disastrous Results of Condom Distribution Programs," by John D. Hartigan. This article adapted and reprinted with permission from *In Focus*, November 1997, the Family Research Council, Washington, D.C.

based and school-linked condom dispensation programs never succeed. Instead of reducing pregnancies, they almost always do just the opposite. To illustrate, consider the outcomes of three highly revealing studies conducted in major U.S. cities:

• *San Francisco*—Even though students were exposed to "graphic demonstrations" of proper condom use,[4] the Balboa High School condom availability program turned out to be a colossal failure. The percentage of sexually active students using condoms almost doubled,[5] but, despite that supposedly positive change in student sexual behavior, the school's overall pregnancy rate increased by one-fourth.[6] With an increase in pregnancy, it can be assumed that there was a similar increase in student exposure to HIV infection and other sexually-transmitted diseases.

• *St. Paul and Dallas*—In two school-based programs that dispensed condoms rather than coupons, the results were even worse than those in San Francisco. Specifically, a St. Paul program that was supposed to reduce annual teenage births actually caused them to spiral upward by one-third (from 22 per 1,000 to 29 per 1,000).[7] An inner-city Dallas school that distributed condoms ended up with an 11.2 percent overall pregnancy rate, 47 percent higher than the 7.6 percent overall pregnancy rate found in an almost identical Dallas school that did not implement such a program.[8]

Moreover, it is folly to believe that dispensing condoms to teenagers might work better if accompanied by expert counseling on how to use

Women Receiving Counseling	Outcome
68 mainly black and Hispanic U.S. women aged 18 to 65 with stable sex partners	7.9 percent of condoms slipped off during intercourse or broke during intercourse or withdrawal. Of the remaining condoms, 7.2 percent slipped off during withdrawal.[9]
18 uninfected adult Florida women with HIV-positive sex partners	Three of the women (16 percent of the cohort) became HIV-infected within 18 months.[10]
31 uninfected adult French women with HIV-positive sex partners	17 of these women "did not adhere to the use of condoms," and three of them were infected.[11]
404 uninfected adult European women with HIV-positive sex partners	Only 49 of these women used condoms all or most of the time, and six of those 49 were infected.[12]
163 uninfected adult European women with HIV-positive sex partners	74 of these women failed to use condoms consistently, and eight of these 74 were infected.[13]

condoms without mishap. As the previous summary indicates, efforts to bring about effective condom use through intensive counseling have proved uniformly unsuccessful, even when the persons being counseled are adult females who are very strongly motivated to avoid pregnancy and HIV infection.

Given this long record of failure, the time has come for educators and health officials to abandon their blind faith in condoms and face the fact that supplying youngsters with condoms does not reduce teenage pregnancies or HIV infections. On the contrary, all the available evidence shows that condom distribution will only worsen the consequences of teenagers' sexual activity. Clearly, another approach needs to be taken if our young people are going to be protected from the scourges of teen pregnancy, sexually-transmitted diseases, and HIV.

Notes

1. Elise F. Jones and Jacqueline D. Forrest, "Contraceptive Failure Rates Based on the 1988 NSFG," *Family Planning Perspectives,* January/February 1992, pages 12–19. See Table 2, page 15.

2. Douglas Kirby, *et al., An Assessment of Six School-Based Clinics: Services, Impact and Potential* (Center for Population Options, 1989), pp. 32, 65; and "Six School-Based Clinics: Their Reproductive Health Services and Impact on Sexual Behavior," *Family Planning Perspectives,* January/February 1991, pp. 6–16, at pp. 11–12. For brevity, the earlier of these Kirby studies is hereafter cited as the "1989 Report" and the more recent as the "1991 Report."

3. Dominique Hausser and P.A. Michaud, "Does a Condom-Promoting Strategy (the Swiss STOP-AIDS Campaign) Modify Sexual Behavior Among Adolescents?" *Pediatrics,* April 1994, Table 3, p. 582.

4. 1989 Report, p. 65.

5. 1989 Report, p. 64.

6. Before the condom coupon experiment began, 37 percent of the school's female students were sexually active, and the annual pregnancy rate was 5.9 percent per year (i.e., 37% × 16%). When the experiment ended two years later, 46 percent of the school's female students were sexually active, and the annual pregnancy rate among these girls was 16 percent, so the school's overall pregnancy rate was 7.4 percent per year (i.e., 46% × 16%, or one-fourth higher than when the experiment started). See 1991 Report, Table 3, p. 11, and Table 8, p. 15.

7. Douglas Kirby, *et al.,* "The Effects of School-Based Health Clinics in St. Paul on School-Wide Birthrates," *Family Planning Perspectives,* January/ February 1993, pp. 12–16. See Table 2, p. 15.

8. At the end of the two-year experiment, 80 percent of the girls in the school that dispensed condoms were sexually active, and the annual pregnancy rate was 11.2 percent per year (i.e., 80% × 14%). By contrast, only 76 percent of the girls in the school that did not dispense condoms had ever engaged in sex, and the annual pregnancy rate among these girls was only 10 percent, so the school's overall pregnancy rate was only 7.6 percent per year (i.e., 76% × 10%). Thus, the overall pregnancy rate in the school that dispensed condoms was 1.47 times the overall pregnancy

rate in the otherwise identical sister school that did not dispense condoms. See 1991 Report, Table 3, p. 11, and Table 8, p. 15.

9. James Trussell, *et al.,* "Condom Slippage and Breakage Rates," *Family Planning Perspectives,* January/February 1992, pp. 20–23. See p. 20 and Table 1, p. 22.

10. Margaret Fischl, *et al.,* "Heterosexual Transmission of Human Immunodeficiency Virus (HIV): Relationship of Sexual Practices to Seroconversion," Third International Conference on AIDS, June 1987, *Abstracts Volume,* p. 178.

11. Y. Laurian, *et al.,* "HIV Infection in Sexual Partners of HIV-Seropositive Patients With Hemophilia," *New England Journal of Medicine,* January 19, 1989, p. 183.

12. European Study Group on Heterosexual Transmission of HIV, "Comparison of female to male and male to female transmission of HIV in stable couples," *British Medical Journal,* March 28, 1992, pp. 809–813. See Table 1, p. 810.

13. Isabelle de Vicenzi, *et al.,* "A Longitudinal Study of Human Immunodeficiency Virus Transmission by Heterosexual Partners," *New England Journal of Medicine,* August 11, 1994, pp. 341–346. See p. 343.

17

Distributing Condoms in Schools Does Not Encourage Teen Sex

Lynda Richardson

Lynda Richardson is a staff writer for the New York Times.

A study that compared the rates of condom use and sexual activity by high school students in schools in New York City and Chicago found that making condoms easily accessible did not increase the rate of teen sex. Students in New York City schools, which have been providing condoms to students as part of an HIV education program, had similar rates of sexual activity as students in Chicago schools, which do not have a condom distribution program.

A study says that making condoms easily accessible to public high school students through AIDS education programs does not increase rates of sexual activity, but it does increase condom use.

The study compared the rates of condom use and sexual activity by thousands of high school students in New York City schools, which offer condoms, and by students in Chicago, where H.I.V./AIDS education is provided, but condoms are not made available in schools. The study concluded that condom access in schools is "a low-cost, harmless addition" to AIDS prevention efforts.

An incendiary topic

AIDS education and condoms in the schools have been incendiary topics across the country, dividing school boards, parents and educators along philosophical, religious and political lines.

The New York City program contributed to the ouster of Schools Chancellor Joseph A. Fernandez, who began it in 1991 as a way of preventing AIDS among teen-agers. More than 400 public schools in 50 districts nationwide make condoms accessible.

Reprinted, with permission, from "Condoms in School Said Not to Affect Teen-Age Sex," by Lynda Richardson, *The New York Times*, September 30, 1997.

The study's findings were published in the September 1997 issue of *The American Journal of Public Health,* a scholarly journal published by the American Public Health Association, a professional organization. The findings rebut the most visceral criticism leveled by opponents of school-based condom programs: that having condoms widely available might make teen-agers more promiscuous.

"This is not a panacea, but it is cheap," said Sally Guttmacher, the lead author and an associate professor at New York University's department of health studies in the School of Education. "It doesn't do any harm and it reaches those kids who most need to be reached."

The study is part of a three-year evaluation of New York City's AIDS Education program financed primarily by the Robert Wood Johnson Foundation and conducted by N.Y.U. researchers. The other researchers were David Ward and Lisa Lieberman.

Experts in adolescent health said the study is the largest assessment yet published of a program that makes condoms available through the schools. It joins a growing body of evidence that indicates that offering condoms in the schools does not increase the level of sexual activity of teen-agers.

One Federal researcher called the study significant. "It's an important study and important findings, but we need many more studies to access efforts to help young people who do engage in intercourse to protect them from being infected," said Lloyd Kolbe, the director of the division of adolescent and school health at the Federal Centers for Disease Control and Prevention in Atlanta.

About a quarter of the 40,000 new H.I.V. infections each year occur among 13-to-21-year-olds. Three million new infections of other sexually transmitted diseases occur annually among 13-to-19-year-olds.

In New York, advocates for prevention programs said they hoped the study would increase pressure on Schools Chancellor Rudy Crew and the Board of Education to increase support for the condom program, which they say has progressively weakened since the departure of its champion, Mr. Fernandez, in 1992.

Making condoms easily accessible to public high school students through AIDS education programs does not increase rates of sexual activity.

The study found that sexually active students in New York were significantly more likely to have used a condom during their most recent act of intercourse than were sexually active students in Chicago. The New York students who had three or more partners within the last six months—nearly 1 in 10 of all high school students—were even more likely to have used a condom during the most recent act than were their counterparts in Chicago, the study found.

The research involved 7,000 students in 12 randomly selected New York City high schools and 6,000 students from 10 demographically similar schools in Chicago. The figures were collected during the 1994–95 academic year.

The study provides the first independent evaluation of the impact of New York's condom program on students.

Mr. Fernandez, the former chancellor in New York City who is now an education consultant based in Miami, said the study gives credence to what he was attempting to do. "It's a wake-up call," he said.

Other collaborators include Alice Radosh of the Academy for Educational Development in Manhattan, a nonprofit research group that conducts education projects; Nick Freudenberg of the Hunter College Center on AIDS, Drugs and Community Health, and Don Des Jarlais of the Chemical Dependency Institute at Beth Israel Medical Center.

Ms. Guttmacher's father was Alan Guttmacher, for whom an institute concerned with reproductive health care is named. The institute did not finance the project. Ms. Guttmacher said her father's views did not influence her during the study.

The Schools Chancellor, Dr. Crew, declined to discuss the study. "Everybody wants to take a good hard look at the study before we offer any comment," said a school system spokesman, J.D. Rock.

The president of the New York City Board of Education, William C. Thompson Jr., said the study could only be helpful. "What a study like this does is encourage principals and individuals within the schools to make sure policy is being followed," Mr. Thompson said.

The findings

While the study shows that less than one-fifth of sexually active New York students reported getting a condom from school, students who had more frequent sex reported getting a condom from school more often than students who had less sex.

The study found that 59.7 percent of New York students and 60.1 percent of Chicago students were sexually active. Of those who were engaged in sex, 60.8 percent of the New Yorkers used a condom during last intercourse, versus 55.5 percent of the Chicagoans.

Some experts say that more studies need to be done before such findings are considered definitive. Various studies have found that schools with condom programs do not experience an increase in sexual activity, but research is still mixed on whether making condoms available in schools actually increases their use, these experts say.

In the New York study, one major limitation was that the researchers were not able to collect data before the systemwide program began. As an alternative, Ms. Guttmacher said, researchers used new students, mostly ninth graders, who had not been exposed to the condom program in New York, and compared them to similar students in Chicago.

The New York findings mirrored research conducted in the Philadelphia schools, said Frank Furstenberg, a sociology professor at the University of Pennsylvania, whose study was published this summer in *Family Planning Perspectives,* a scholarly journal.

"These studies point in the same direction, but we certainly need more evidence," he said. "But if I were a superintendent in a public school considering the effects of the program, I would certainly be confident enough to try this approach."

At least 431 public schools in 50 school districts nationwide make condoms available, which represents 2.2 percent of all public high schools and 0.3 percent of high school districts, said two California researchers, Douglas B. Kirby and Nancy L. Brown, whose survey was published last year in *Family Planning Perspectives*.

In New York City's program, specially trained teachers are supposed to make condoms available to students in special health resource rooms in the city's high schools, along with information about their use and about AIDS. Counseling and referral services are also supposed to be available. The health curriculum is supposed to include six classes a year on how to guard against H.I.V., the virus that causes AIDS.

But there are enormous variations in how the program is carried out, with some high schools embracing the program with posters and rigorous lessons and others having a program only on paper, say the researchers, parents and students.

"It is not being enforced," said Janine Medina, a 17-year-old at East Side Community School on the Lower East Side and a volunteer for an advocacy group that provides information on H.I.V. prevention. "A lot of public high schools don't even have health resource rooms, which are supposed to have condoms available in them."

18

Teen Magazines Encourage Teen Sex

Wendy Shalit

Wendy Shalit is the author of A Return to Modesty: Discovering the Lost Virtue.

While each magazine geared for teens promises to be different, they are all very similar in that they promote and glamorize promiscuity and teen sex. What teens really need is advice on how to set and uphold limits on sexual activity. Teen magazines should concentrate on teaching teens how to develop their full potential rather than how to look and act sexy for the opposite sex.

When you think teen magazines, you probably think of *Seventeen, Glamour* or *YM (Young & Modern)*. Well, you're way behind the times. These days we have *Twist* (Bauer Publishing Co.), *Girl* (Lewit & LeWinter) and even *Latingirl* (MicroMedia Affiliates), an English-language publication trying to break into the Hispanic teen market.

While *Twist* offers tips on getting a guy ("How to Read His Secret Love Signals") and *Latingirl* is directed at young readers "who want to maintain their bicultural identity," what appears to be difference really isn't. The front half of these magazines is still devoted to promoting an easy attitude toward sex and the back to curing the problems that this attitude causes (divorce, lack of self-respect, eating disorders and so on). *Girl*, which was pitched as a fashion magazine for "real" (i.e., plumper) girls, has already abandoned its niche idea. As the editors explained, "We decided that since all of you rock, *Girl* would be for everyone—not just one specific type of girl."

Vulgar and jaded

In the battery of cultural messages that assault young women every day—from movies, TV and music to schoolroom sermons and social pressures—the pages of the young women's magazines occupy a strategic position. They offer a glossy display of sophistication and jadedness, and

Reprinted, with permission, from "Youth Wants to Know, but What Are the Young Women's Magazines Telling Them?" by Wendy Shalit, *Wall Street Journal*, March 26, 1999.

they give a glamorous sanction to the sexual revolution. The ideal is to look androgynous and to be tough.

Of course it is not only the new mags that send these messages. The old standbys are equally vulgar. This March [1999], *YM* treats girls to "A Day in the Life of a Boy's Boxers." The April 1999 issue of *Seventeen* runs almost the same article in its "Sex + Body All About Him" section. But girls don't really need another lecture on the physiology of puberty; they want what they never get in sex-ed classes—advice.

The questions they ask are still as earnest as ever, like this one in *Mademoiselle* (one of the many magazines aimed at twentysomethings that teens read): "College is a time to experiment, right? So if I practice safe sex and choose partners I trust, is it okay to sleep around?" Comes the reply, as ironic as they have come to expect: "Okay with whom, me? Sure."

The closest thing to advice girls ever get in these magazines is in *YM*'s April 1999 edition, where it issues a call to "get cybersexy." In *Seventeen*, twins Alexsandra and Brittany are deemed too "conservative" and so are made up to look like Gwyneth Paltrow and Cameron Diaz. Before the makeover they looked like fresh-faced 14-year-olds; after it, they look pseudo-sophisticated and profoundly unhappy.

And with good reason. The March 1999 issue of *Pediatrics*—not exactly on most teens' reading list although it should be on their parents'—reports that the more a girl reads these magazines, the more likely she is to think of herself as unattractive and overweight (even if she isn't).

Every new women's magazine begins with promises of being "different" and ends up just as bad as the rest. Jane Pratt's newest magazine—she edited *Savvy* a few years ago—was supposed to provide a serious alternative to the typical young women's magazine. To judge by its Jan/Feb 1999 issue, though, things are not going well. Here *Jane* elects Monica Lewinsky one of "The 10 Gutsiest Women of the Year" because "most get intimidated by concepts like Sex With Pres; Monica doesn't."

Also in *Jane*, we find tips on "Horizontal Beauty"—that is, how to improve the "early morning you." That sounds harmless enough, but *Jane* has something else in mind: "Those first few sleepovers," the article notes, "are always a tad anxiety-ridden." Not for the reasons you might expect, however. The big question the morning after you've slept with a new guy is, "Are your bangs defying gravity?" Luckily, we are told, if we dot Max Factor's Erace Secret Cover-Up and Cover Girl's extra-smudgeproof mascara on before falling asleep, we can be lovely upon awaking and our bedmate will be less likely to sprint away from us.

But if our bedmate can't understand messy hair and smudged mascara in the morning, should we really be sleeping with him in the first place? Should we be sleeping with him in any case? About this, *Jane* offers no comment.

A new generation

Just when you thought the young women's magazine market couldn't be more saturated, a whole new generation of girl gazettes is emerging. After *Teen People,* a junior version of *People,* secured a circulation bigger than *Vogue* in its first year, *Newsweek* announced its plans for *Teen Newsweek* and Hearst its plans for a teen magazine based on *Cosmopolitan.* A *Teen*

Cosmo should be interesting. One can already imagine the headlines: "Playground Hang-Ups Solved! Boy Pulls Down Your Skirt in Front of Friends: Try Our New Butterfly Position!" And Helen Gurley Brown can offer tips to preteens on how to be such a fantastic sleeping-bag partner that he'll never want to leave you.

It's not hard to see why publisher Sherry Handel used her savings in 1996 to found *Blue Jean,* a take-no-advertising publication for teen girls that attempted to address some of their real concerns. Unfortunately, her venture didn't last. *Jump* is the most promising of the new teen magazines, with its features on girls who volunteer and who actually believe in things. In its April 1999 issue we meet Ceilidh Yurenka, age 16, who ran a campaign to stop frog dissection at her New Hampshire school. But ending frog dissection is not a compelling enough alternative to an obsession with one's physical appearance.

The front half of [teen] magazines is still devoted to promoting an easy attitude toward sex and the back to curing the problems that this attitude causes.

Generally speaking, the message that girls are more than their outfits won't come from teen magazines, which are peddling those outfits. And don't expect it to come from the Girl Scouts, either. They now offer a "From Fitness to Fashion" patch, featuring a little black dress, a lipstick and compact case, and a barbell. You earn it only after you have "learned the meaning of the following skincare terms: hypoallergenic, toner, astringent" and after having studied the masthead of your favorite fashion magazine. A Girl Scout in New Haven, Conn., defends the patch in *Allure* magazine by arguing that "it helps you to learn types of makeup."

The problem is that since the 1960s we have found it "sexist" to expect girls to be morally good—no more eternal feminine, woman-on-a-pedestal business here. So now the only womanly things left for them to be good at are putting on lipstick and being good . . . in bed. The tyranny of the superficial feminine won't end until we revive, unironically and unapologetically, the notion of feminine virtue and give girls metaphysical goals to aspire to: intelligence, patience, self-sacrifice, temperance and perhaps a little modesty.

Those things have got to be at least as patch-worthy as lipstick.

19

Television Influences Teen Attitudes Toward Sex

Gina R. Dalfonzo

Gina R. Dalfonzo is a writer at the Family Research Council.

Teens see an extraordinary amount of sexual imagery on television; two-thirds of television shows contain some sexual content, and those shows depict more than four sex scenes per hour. Television rarely shows examples of sexual morality or encourages teens to remain abstinent. Nor does television depict the very real feelings of self-doubt, guilt, and unhappiness that often accompany sexual intimacy. Parents should talk with their teenagers about relationships and moral guidelines.

In case your son or daughter has a habit of turning off the popular teen soap opera *Dawson's Creek* when you walk in, here's what you've been missing.

In [one] episode, after months of obsessing about whether to "go all the way" with boyfriend Pacey, the 17-year-old character Joey finally decided it was time. Accompanied by romantic music (not to mention the shrieking of adolescents all across America), the couple broke out the condom and started undressing each other as the screen faded to black.

If the thought of your child watching this scene bothers you, you're out of touch. After all, these two high school seniors had waited nine months already and waiting for marriage was never part of their plan anyway. The show's executive producer Paul Stupin said, "It was time to address this issue. If we are going to depict an honest relationship and show in a truthful way how a relationship between these two people progresses, sex has to be dealt with."

Joey, in fact, is supposed to be a heroine because she waited for exactly "the right moment." The moral of her story goes something like this: Wait for sex until you're sure it's true love. Or until it's TV's big sweeps week, when your bosses at the network count on you for some really good ratings.

Reprinted, with permission, from "The New Sexual Morality," by Gina R. Dalfonzo, *Daily Journal*, February 27, 2001.

Sex on television

But seriously, what does it matter if two kids have sex on television? Teenagers know it's all fantasy, right? Actually, it would be surprising if they did, considering the amount of sexual imagery they see every day. As the Kaiser Family Foundation reported, about two-thirds of TV shows contain some sexual content; those shows feature "an average of 4.1 scenes per hour involving sex."

On teen shows in particular, the same scenario repeats endlessly: Boy meets girl. Boy and girl date a while. Girl visits clinic and gets a stern but kindly lecture and a handful of birth control paraphernalia. Boy and girl "go all the way." And usually, in the next few episodes, boy and girl part ways and start looking for other partners. (Rumor has it that such a breakup already is planned for *Dawson's Creek*'s passionate pair.) Examples of sexual morality are almost nonexistent. When a character on the college drama *Felicity* declared his intention to save sex for marriage, it took his girlfriend all of three episodes to break down his resolve.

Few and far between are characters like Nicole, a teenager in the new film *Going the Distance*. After almost going too far with her boyfriend, Phil, Nicole looks at him and says simply, "I wanted you to but I'm really glad we didn't." Acknowledging it's going to be difficult, the two nevertheless decide to stick it out and remain chaste. But for every "Nicole and Phil" encouraging kids to abstain from premarital sex, there are at least six or seven "Joey and Paceys" suggesting they go for it.

Sad to say, pop culture is only reinforcing the lessons taught by teachers and other authority figures. Author and educator Evelyn Lerman titled her recent book *Safer Sex: The New Morality*, summing up the way many sex educators and health organizations view teen sex. Lerman suggests a "new morality" based on these ideas: "Abstain from early sex if possible. Abstain from giving or getting sexually transmitted infections. Abstain from having unplanned babies. Abstain from the need for an abortion."

About two-thirds of TV shows contain some sexual content; those shows feature "an average of 4.1 scenes per hour involving sex."

In short, morality now means waiting until you're sure you're in love and then using a condom. And the only "sin" is getting sick or pregnant. If this is the test for morality, *Dawson's Creek* passes easily. It has even won an award from The Media Project, an organization that honors "accurate portrayals of family planning, sexuality and reproductive health." But in real life, the *Dawson's Creek* scenario flunks out. For one thing, it makes "safe sex" look safer than it is. In the picture-perfect world of teen television, there's no such thing as a defective or torn condom, or a disease like human papillomavirus that can get past a condom.

Even worse, such shows ignore the very real feelings of self-doubt and unhappiness that premarital sex brings with it. Abstinence educator Emily Chase recalls seeing girls come into her local crisis pregnancy center for pregnancy tests: "Often the test results were negative; the girl was not pregnant. But the hurts of the broken relationships, the guilt they felt about having breached their boundaries remained."

But with "the new morality," no one is supposed to feel guilt. One of Joey's friends advises her, "Has it ever occurred to you that you might be so caught up trying to find the right choice that you never really stop to think about the possibility that there may not be the right choice or the wrong choice? Just a bunch of choices?

There's nothing to figure out here. It's only what you feel."

Aside from terrible writing, the problem with that advice is that it's unrealistic. It leaves teenagers with no moral foundation, no reason to listen to the voice of conscience—and in the end, no basis for self-respect. Parents who truly want to be honest with their teenagers about relationships would be well advised to turn off the teen soap operas and sit down for a talk about moral guidelines. Kids need to know even though "the new morality" may seem exciting and glamorous, it only works on television.

Organizations to Contact

The editors have compiled the following list of organizations concerned with the issues debated in this book. The descriptions are derived from materials provided by the organizations. All have publications or information available for interested readers. The list was compiled on the date of publication of the present volume; the information provided here may change. Be aware that many organizations take several weeks or longer to respond to inquiries, so allow as much time as possible.

Advocates for Youth
1025 Vermont Ave. NW, Suite 200, Washington, DC 20005
(202) 347-5700 • fax: (202) 347-2263
e-mail: info@advocatesforyouth.org • website: www.advocatesforyouth.org

Advocates for Youth is the only national organization focusing solely on pregnancy and HIV prevention among young people. It provides information, education, and advocacy to youth-serving agencies and professionals, policymakers, and the media. Among the organization's numerous publications are the brochures *Advice from Teens on Buying Condoms* and *Spread the Word—Not the Virus* and the pamphlet *How to Prevent Date Rape: Teen Tips.*

Alan Guttmacher Institute
120 Wall St., 21st Floor, New York, NY 10005
(212) 248-1111 • fax: (212) 248-1951
e-mail: info@agi-usa.org • website: www.agi-usa.org

The institute works to protect and expand the reproductive choices of all women and men. It strives to ensure that people have access to the information and services they need to exercise their rights and responsibilities concerning sexual activity, reproduction, and family planning. Among the institute's publications are the books *Teenage Pregnancy in Industrialized Countries* and *Today's Adolescents, Tomorrow's Parents: A Portrait of the Americas* and the report "Sex and America's Teenagers."

Centers for Disease Control and Prevention (CDC)
National Center for HIV, STD, and TB Prevention
1108 Corporate Square, Atlanta, GA 30329
(404) 639-8040 • fax: (888) 232-3299
e-mail: nchstp@cdc.gov • website: www.cdc.gov/nchstp

The CDC is the government agency charged with protecting the public health of the nation by preventing and controlling diseases and by responding to public health emergencies. The National Center for HIV, STD, and TB Prevention (NCHSTP) works to prevent and control human immunodeficiency virus infection, sexually transmitted diseases, and tuberculosis. NCHSTP publishes the fact sheets "STDs and Pregnancy" and "Trends in Sexual Risk Behaviors Among High School Students" and provides a free fax service for information on HIV and STDs.

Child Trends, Inc. (CT)
4301 Connecticut Ave. NW, Suite 100, Washington, DC 20008
(202) 362-5580 • fax: (202) 362-5533
e-mail: swilliams@childtrends.org • website: www.childtrends.org

CT works to provide accurate statistical and research information regarding children and their families in the United States and to educate the American public on the ways existing social trends, such as the increasing rate of teenage pregnancy, affect children. In addition to the annual newsletter *Facts at a Glance*, which presents the latest data on teen pregnancy rates for every state, CT also publishes the papers "Next-Steps and Best Bets: Approaches to Preventing Adolescent Childbearing" and "Welfare and Adolescent Sex: The Effects of Family History, Benefit Levels, and Community Context."

Coalition for Positive Sexuality (CPS)
3712 N. Broadway, PMB #191, Chicago, IL 60613
(773) 604-1654
website: www.positive.org

The Coalition for Positive Sexuality is a grassroots direct-action group formed in the spring of 1992 by high school students and activists. CPS works to counteract the institutionalized misogyny, heterosexism, homophobia, racism, and ageism that students experience every day at school. It is dedicated to offering teens sexuality and safe sex education that is pro-woman, pro-lesbian/gay/bisexual, pro-safe sex, and pro-choice. Its motto is, "Have fun and be safe." CPS publishes the pamphlet *Just Say Yes*.

Concerned Women for America (CWA)
370 L'Enfant Promenade SW, Suite 800, Washington, DC 20024
(202) 488-7000 • fax: (202) 488-0806
website: www.cwfa.org

CWA's purpose is to preserve, protect, and promote traditional Judeo-Christian values through education, legislative action, and other activities. It is concerned with creating an environment that is conducive to building strong families and raising healthy children. CWA publishes the monthly *Family Voice*, which periodically addresses such issues as promoting sexual abstinence in schools.

Family Research Council (FRC)
801 G St. NW, Washington, DC 20001
(202) 393-2100 • fax: (202) 393-2134
e-mail: corrdept@frc.org • website: www.frc.org

The council is a research, resource, and education organization that promotes the traditional family, which the council defines as a group of people bound by marriage, blood, or adoption. It opposes schools' tolerance of homosexuality and condom distribution programs in schools. It also believes that pornography breaks up marriages and contributes to sexual violence. Among the council's numerous publications are the papers "Revolt of the Virgins," "Abstinence: The New Sexual Revolution," and "Abstinence Programs Show Promise in Reducing Sexual Activity and Pregnancy Among Teens."

Focus on the Family
Colorado Springs, CO 80995
(719) 531-5181 • fax: (719) 531-3424
website: www.fotf.org

Focus on the Family is an organization that promotes Christian values and strong family ties and that campaigns against pornography and homosexual rights laws. It publishes the monthly magazine *Focus on the Family* and the books *Love Won Out: A Remarkable Journey Out of Homosexuality* and *No Apologies . . . the Truth About Life, Love, and Sex.*

The Heritage Foundation
214 Massachusetts Ave. NE, Washington, DC 20002-4999
(202) 546-4400 • fax: (202) 546-8328
e-mail: info@heritage.org • website: www.heritage.org

The Heritage Foundation is a public policy research institute that supports the ideas of limited government and the free-market system. It promotes the view that the welfare system has contributed to the problems of illegitimacy and teenage pregnancy. Among the foundation's numerous publications is its Backgrounder series, which includes "Liberal Welfare Programs: What the Data Show on Programs for Teenage Mothers," the paper "Rising Illegitimacy: America's Social Catastrophe," and the bulletin "How Congress Can Protect the Rights of Parents to Raise Their Children."

National Campaign to Prevent Teen Pregnancy
21 M St. NW, Suite 300, Washington, DC 20037
(202) 261-5655
website: www.teenpregnancy.org

The mission of the National Campaign is to reduce teenage pregnancy by promoting values and activities that are consistent with a pregnancy-free adolescence. The campaign's goal is to reduce the pregnancy rate among teenage girls by one-third by the year 2005. The campaign publishes pamphlets, brochures, and opinion polls that include *No Easy Answers: Research Findings on Programs to Reduce Teen Pregnancy, Not Just for Girls: Involving Boys and Men in Teen Pregnancy Prevention,* and *Public Opinion Polls and Teen Pregnancy.*

National Organization on Adolescent Pregnancy, Parenting, and Prevention (NOAPPP)
2401 Pennsylvania Ave., Suite 350, Washington, DC 20037
(202) 293-8370
e-mail: noappp@noappp.org • website: www.noappp.org

NOAPPP promotes comprehensive and coordinated services designed for the prevention and resolution of problems associated with adolescent pregnancy and parenthood. It supports families in setting standards that encourage the healthy development of children through loving, stable relationships. NOAPPP publishes the quarterly *NOAPPP Network Newsletter* and various fact sheets on teen pregnancy.

Planned Parenthood Federation of America (PPFA)
810 7th Ave., New York, NY 10019
(212) 541-7800 • fax: (212) 245-1845
e-mail: communications@ppfa.org • website: www.plannedparenthood.org

Planned Parenthood believes individuals have the right to control their own fertility without governmental interference. It promotes comprehensive sex education and provides contraceptive counseling and services through clinics across the United States. Its publications include the brochures *Guide to Birth Control: Seven Accepted Methods of Contraception* and *Teen Sex? It's Okay to Say No Way,* and the bimonthly newsletter *LinkLine.*

Project Reality
PO Box 97, Golf, IL 60029-0097
(847) 729-3298
e-mail: preality@pair.com • website: www.project-reality.pair.com

Project Reality has developed a sex education curriculum for junior and senior high students called Sex Respect. The program is designed to provide teenagers with information and to encourage sexual abstinence.

Sex Information and Education Council of Canada (SIECCAN)
850 Coxwell Ave., Toronto, ON M4C 5R1 Canada
(416) 466-5304 • fax: (416) 778-0785
e-mail: sieccan@web.net • website: www.sieccan.org

SIECCAN conducts research on sexual health and sexuality education. It publishes *The Canadian Journal of Human Sexuality* and the resource document *Common Questions About Sexual Health Education*, and maintains an information service for health professionals.

Sexuality Information and Education Council of the United States (SIECUS)
130 W. 42nd St., Suite 350, New York, NY 10036-7802
(212) 819-9770 • fax: (212) 819-9776
e-mail: siecus@siecus.org • website: www.siecus.org

SIECUS is an organization of educators, physicians, social workers, and others who support the individual's right to acquire knowledge of sexuality and who encourage responsible sexual behavior. The council promotes comprehensive sex education for all children that includes AIDS education, teaching about homosexuality, and instruction about contraceptives and sexually transmitted diseases. Its publications include fact sheets, annotated bibliographies by topic, the booklet *Talk About Sex*, and the monthly *SIECUS Report.*

Teen-Aid
723 E. Jackson Ave., Spokane, WA 99207
(509) 482-2868 • fax: (509) 482-7994
e-mail: teenaid@teen-aid.org • website: www.teen-aid.org

Teen-Aid is an international organization that promotes traditional family values and sexual morality. It publishes a public school sex education curriculum, *Sexuality, Commitment, and Family*, stressing sexual abstinence before marriage.

Bibliography

Books

Bill Ameiss and Jane Graver	*Love, Sex, and God*. St. Louis, MO: Concordia Publishing House, 1998.
Nathalie Bartle with Susan Lieberman	*Venus in Blue Jeans: Why Mothers and Daughters Need to Talk About Sex*. Boston: Houghton Mifflin, 1998.
Michael J. Basso	*The Underground Guide to Teenage Sexuality: An Essential Handbook for Today's Teens and Parents*. Minneapolis: Fairview Press, 1997.
Janet Bode	*Kids Still Having Kids: Talking About Teen Pregnancy*. Rev. ed. Danbury, CT: Franklin Watts, 1999.
Robert W. Buckingham and Mary P. Derby	*"I'm Pregnant, Now What Do I Do?"* Amherst, NY: Prometheus Books, 1997.
Mary Ann Cantwell	*Homosexuality: The Secret a Child Dare Not Tell*. San Rafael, CA: Rafael Press, 1996.
Julie Endersbe	*Homosexuality: What Does It Mean?* Mankato, MN: Life-Matters, 2000.
E. James Lieberman and Karen Lieberman Troccoli	*Like It Is: A Teen Sex Guide*. Jefferson, NC: McFarland, 1998.
Jeanne Warren Lindsay	*Pregnant? Adoption Is an Option: Making an Adoption Plan for a Child*. Buena Park, CA: Morning Glory Press, 1997.
Mike A. Males	*Framing Youth: Ten Myths About the Next Generation*. Monroe, ME: Common Courage Press, 1999.
Mike A. Males	*The Scapegoat Generation: America's War on Adolescents*. Monroe, ME: Common Courage Press, 1996.
Ronald Filiberti Moglia and Jon Knowles, eds.	*All About Sex: A Family Resource on Sex and Sexuality*. New York: Crown, 1997.
Robert E. Owens Jr.	*Queer Kids: The Challenges and Promise for Lesbian, Gay, and Bisexual Youth*. New York: Haworth Press, 1998.
Richard A. Panzer	*Condom Nation: Blind Faith, Bad Science*. Westwood, NJ: Center for Educational Media, 1997.
Susan Browning Pogany	*SexSmart: 501 Reasons to Hold Off on Sex*. Minneapolis: Fairview Press, 1998.
Lynn E. Ponton	*The Sex Lives of Teenagers: Revealing the Secret World of Adolescent Boys and Girls*. New York: Dutton, 2000.

Ritch C. Savin-Williams	*Mom, Dad, I'm Gay: How Families Negotiate Coming Out.* Washington, DC: American Psychological Association, 2001.
Michael A. Sommers and Annie Leah Sommers	*Everything You Need to Know About Virginity.* New York: Rosen, 2000.
Joe White	*Pure Excitement: A Radical Righteous Approach to Sex, Love, and Dating.* Wheaton, IL: Tyndale House, 1996.
Neil and Briar Whitehead	*My Genes Made Me Do It! A Scientific Look at Sexual Orientation.* Lafayette, LA: Huntington House, 1999.
Naomi Wolf	*Promiscuities: The Secret Struggle for Womanhood.* New York: Random House, 1997.

Periodicals

Bob Bartlett	"Intimacy 101 for Teens," *U.S. Catholic*, August 1999.
John Cloud	"Out, Proud, and Very Young," *Time*, December 8, 1997.
Amy Dickinson	"Teenage Sex," *Time*, November 8, 1999.
Jennifer Egan	"Lonely Gay Teen Seeking Same," *New York Times Magazine*, December 10, 2000.
Gary J. Gates and Freya L. Sonenstein	"Heterosexual Genital Sexual Activity Among Adolescent Males: 1988 and 1995," *Family Planning Perspectives*, November/December 2000.
Sally Guttmacher et al.	"Condom Availability in New York City Public High Schools," *American Journal of Public Health*, September 1997.
Bobby Jindal	"Medicine and Political Control," *Culture Wars*, April 1997.
Douglas Kirby et al.	"The Impact of Condom Distribution in Seattle Schools on Sexual Behavior and Condom Use," *American Journal of Public Health*, February 1999.
Tamar Lewin	"Survey Shows Sex Practices of Boys," *New York Times*, December 19, 2000.
David Lipsky	"To Be Young and Gay," *Rolling Stone*, August 6, 1998.
Susan McClelland	"Not So Hot to Trot," *Maclean's*, April 9, 2001.
Celia Milne	"Sex and the Single Teen," *Maclean's*, December 28, 1998.
Newsweek	"The Naked Truth," May 8, 2000.
People Weekly	"Growing Up Gay," August 17, 1998.
Karen S. Peterson	"Younger Kids Trying It Now, Often Ignorant of Risks," *USA Today*, November 16, 2000.
Lisa Remez	"Oral Sex Among Adolescents: Is It Sex or Abstinence?" *Family Planning Perspectives*, November 2000.

Diana Jean Schemo   "Sex Education with Just One Lesson: No Sex," *New York Times*, December 28, 2000.

Diana Jean Schemo   "What Teenagers Talk About When They Talk About Chastity," *New York Times*, January 28, 2001.

Mark A. Schuster et al.   "Impact of a High School Condom Availability Program on Sexual Attitudes and Behaviors," *Family Planning Perspectives*, March/April 1998.

Ron Stodghill II   "Where'd You Learn That?" *Time*, June 15, 1998.

Victor C. Strasburger   "Tuning In to Teenagers," *Newsweek*, May 19, 1997.

Gary Thomas   "Where True Love Waits," *Christianity Today*, March 1, 1999.

Michelle Towner, as told to Stephanie Booth   "I'm HIV Positive," *Teen*, October 1999.

David Whitman, Paul Glastris, and Brendan I. Koerner   "Was It Good for Us?" *U.S. News & World Report*, May 19, 1997.

Index